First published in 2011 by Voyageur Press, an imprint of MBI Publishing Company, 400 First Avenue North, Suite 300, Minneapolis, MN 55401 USA

Voyageur Press titles are also available at discounts in bulk quantity for industrial or sales-promotional use. For details write to Special Sales Manager at MBI Publishing Company, 400 First Avenue North, Suite 300, Minneapolis, MN 55401 USA.

To find out more about our books, visit us online at www.voyageurpress.com.

ISBN-13: 978-0-7603-3820-9

Library of Congress Cataloging-in-Publication Data

Lalley, Heather, 1975-
  The Chicago homegrown cookbook : local food, local restaurants, local recipes / Heather Lalley ; photographs by Brendan Lekan.
     p. cm.
  ISBN 978-0-7603-3820-9
  1. Cooking—Illinois—Chicago. 2. Cooking, America—Midwestern style. 3. Cookbooks. I. Title.
  TX715.2.M53L34 2011
  641.59773'11--dc22
                              2010040875

Editor: Kari Cornell
Design Manager: Katie Sonmor
Design: Ellen Huber
Layout: Karl Laun

Printed in China

The Chicago Homegrown Cookbook

Local Food, Local Restaurants, Local Recipes

By Heather Lalley
Photography by Brendan Lekan

Voyageur Press

contents

summer

fall

winter

Foreword

Chef Erwin Drechsler is a farm-to-table pioneer in Chicago. A product of the city's northwest side, he grew up in a house focused on local and seasonal foods. His parents tended a huge backyard vegetable garden, bursting with strawberries, tomatoes, zucchini, and even currant bushes.

Drechsler's father, a meatpacker, would bring home fresh cuts of meat to grind into hamburger. He'd buy fresh chicken and duck from the live-poultry store.

Years later, that fresh, local, seasonal upbringing informed Drechsler's award-winning style of urban-heartland cuisine at his restaurants Metropolis Cafe, Metropolis 1800, and, currently, erwin cafe. He became one of the first chefs to shop the city's newborn farmers' markets for his restaurants.

Along the way, many of Chicago's finest cooks—including some in this book—spent time in Drechsler's kitchen. And all of them credit Drechsler with planting the seed that nurtured their passion for local ingredients.

Each summer for the last decade, Drechsler has led farmers' market tours that culminate with a three-course dinner at this restaurant, prepared with ingredients from the day's shopping.

Here, in his own words, are Drechsler's memories of those early farmers' market days:

Being a chef in Chicago provides me with the bounty of the Midwest, which I have woven into a style of cooking I call "urban-heartland" cuisine. The foundation and core of my cooking is based upon the products provided at local farmers' markets. These local markets in Chicago gave me my early introduction to local Midwest produce, years before the Green City Market came on board.

Going to these markets in Lincoln Park and Evanston the early 1980s was like being a kid in a candy store. In the early days, selection was thin and farmers focused solely on produce—no meat, cheese, eggs, or prepared foods like you see today. But the markets grew fast once farmers realized how deeply their customers appreciated local food.

Markets began the first week of June and, depending on the weather, showcased spring's first produce: pencil asparagus, green garlic, fresh herbs, baby lettuces, and the occasional ramps. Few people talked about organics during these early years. But still, the quality and freshness of the farmers' crops was top notch.

Just as home cooks caught on to the wonders of the market, a growing number of chefs became regulars, too. I remember seeing Rick Bayless choosing produce for his restaurants at some of the first markets.

Another beauty of these early farmers' markets was the seasonal approach they allowed us in preparing our dishes. As we moved from spring to summer and then to fall, our menus reflected the season's crops. We eagerly awaited the first of sugar snap peas, green and wax beans, spring onions, and the season's first strawberry crop, as well as local rhubarb.

Then came tomatoes of every type, and blueberries. There's nothing better than a plate of sliced red and yellow tomatoes with sharp arugula, spring onions, and a drizzle of extra-virgin olive oil. Those blueberries, strawberries, and rhubarb were blended together to form a simple crisp topped with whipped crème fraîche.

Now we were into the heart of summer, and stone fruit began to appear. Peaches, plums, and apricots were as sweet as one can imagine. Peppers, zucchini, and sweet corn rounded out the mix. The sweet perfume of Athena melons and golden raspberries filled the air.

Moving into fall, we were blessed with a wide variety of apples, pears, grapes, and squashes. This provided our restaurant with our famous butternut squash and apple cider soup. Sadly, though, a cold Chicago winter waited in the wings. And the markets drew to a close at October's end.

But for chefs willing to take the time to tour the markets and pick the best of each season, Chicago-area growers provided the bounty of the Midwest and allowed our menus to shine.

Our local farmers' markets have evolved beyond Midwest-grown fruits and vegetables. We now see cheeses from Wisconsin, locally baked breads, honeys and jams, free-range eggs, and local beef and sausages. If it's from the Midwest and you can eat it, it's available for home cooks and restaurant chefs.

To me, all this food evokes memories of robust family dinners, of spirited backyard barbecues, of hearty meals shared with friends, and of the diversified ethnic backgrounds and traditions that have brought us all together in this place.

Now, most every neighborhood has its own farmers' market. And an ever-growing number of chefs now know the importance of local food. The choice is ours to make: local and fresh. Support those who carry on this legacy.

To those farmers who have provided myself and others with the opportunity to serve great-tasting, super-fresh local foods: cheers.

—Erwin Drechsler

Introduction

Local. Seasonal. Sustainable. Farm fresh.

These days, it's hard to pick up a restaurant menu in Chicago that doesn't boast at least one of those adjectives.

But to the farmers and chefs profiled in these pages, these are more than buzzwords. They are a way of life. These are farmers who rise before the roosters to bring fresh produce, meats, and cheeses to area farmers' markets. These are chefs who kick off the day with an early trip to the market and wrap it up in the wee hours of the night, after feeding hundreds of appreciative diners.

Fortunately for Chicago restaurant-goers, it's easy to find chefs in the city committed to featuring locally sourced products. In choosing the chefs spotlighted in this book, we sought out those with the strongest ties to area farmers and those doing the most innovative work with homegrown foods.

Inside, you'll find the stories behind some of Chicago's most buzzworthy chefs: What inspires them? What brought them to the kitchen? What nurtured their passion for locally grown foods? And you'll soak up the personalities of some of the area's most hardworking farmers—superstars in their own right.

Just as these chefs and farmers are governed by the cycle of the seasons, so too is the organization of this book. We've made it easy for you to match your cooking to what's available at the farmers' markets each spring, summer, fall, and winter.

The climate of the Upper Midwest allows for a wonderful bounty of products to be grown, raised, and produced. But, of course, not every food a creative chef might want in his or her palette can be locally sourced. So, you will find some recipes in this book that occasionally call for more exotic ingredients.

We hope that in reading the stories and seeing the faces of these farmers and chefs, you'll strengthen your appreciation for the hard work that goes into creating local, seasonal food. And by trying some of the dozens of outstanding recipes included here, we hope you'll enjoy bringing a little homegrown food into your own kitchen.

spring

Like water to a person in the desert, spring arrives just when we need it. That first warm day sparkles like a jewel. Just as we're tiring of root vegetables, in waltzes arugula and asparagus, and maybe a mojito (or two). Take a sip and savor spring.

You've earned it.

Aria

Chef Chad Starling
Nichols Farm

Success has come to farmer Lloyd Nichols through years of hard work and adherence to a deceptively simple philosophy:

"Our little motto is: Variety is our specialty," Nichols says.

Nichols, his wife, and their three sons grow more than a thousand varieties of fruits and vegetables on their 400-acre farm in Marengo, Illinois. He suspects that makes him the most diversified farmer in the region.

"If you can grow it in this area, we've tried to grow it," he says. Such diversity helps the farm stay profitable even if one crop suffers a bad year, such as tomatoes during a recent blight. It also allows him to experiment with "chancy" crops, such as artichokes, which can be challenging to grow in Illinois' climate.

Years of trial and error plus lots of advance planning have helped the Nichols family learn to keep track of all of those hundreds and hundreds of crops, along with a certain amount of laid-back attitude, Nichols says.

"It would be [stressful] if I was meticulously fanatical about it," he says. "If you've got to cross every T and dot every I, you'd go absolutely berserk."

Biodiversity on the farm has been built over many years. When Nichols and his wife, Doreen, bought the farm in 1977, they started with just four acres of vegetables on a 10-acre patch. The two had both worked at O'Hare Airport and had always had a garden. Lloyd Nichols, who grew up in the Chicago suburbs, even tended a garden as a youngster in the 1950s.

"My dad was a gardener," he says. "That's probably how I got into it. I always had a little garden. Then it just became a big garden."

By 1978, the Nichols began selling their produce at the small number of markets around the area. But things really exploded with the creation of the Green City Market and the growing interest of chefs in locally grown foods.

"The Green City ended up being the most important market in the region, and it took a long time for it to get that way," Nichols says. "The thing that made the Green City Market is that it attracted the chef clientele for the region."

Having three sons interested in the family business allowed the farm to expand as well. Nichols Farm works with about fifty Chicago-area chefs and makes deliveries to restaurants around the area.

"That was the incentive to grow," Nichols says. "Three adult sons and their families. We kept on growing to where we are now. It was a gradual thing over the years."

Chef Chad Starling appreciates the diversity he gets in Nichols' products and has used produce from the farm at all three restaurants in which he has cooked in Chicago.

"They have tons of produce," Starling says. "I have their name listed on my menu."

Starling grew up in Tennessee, where he ran a home-maintenance business. He started cooking to supplement his income and fell in love.

"Growing up in the South, you're surrounded by food," Starling says. "It's just part of the culture. Big meals and farms. And eating the whole animal."

He soaked up every morsel of knowledge he could from the first chef with whom he worked. He went on to cook at a four-star resort in Key West, Florida, before traveling to Asia to do some exploring.

"I just had the need to travel and see the world," he says. "I was equally interested in Asian food and culture. I fell in love with the culture and the food. It became part of what I started doing, culinary-wise."

After his travels, Starling began cooking in Lake Tahoe, an experience that developed his interest in using locally sourced ingredients.

"We had whole lambs brought in to the back door," Starling says.

With local-food innovation on his mind, Starling decided to move to Chicago.

"I came here to cook," he says. "Chicago was at the time, and still is, the new food destination. I wanted to be part of that. Also, the farms out here are incredible."

And now Starling is the chef at Aria, a contemporary Asian restaurant that emphasizes local ingredients.

"My philosophy is clean, fresh ingredients that are really balanced," he says. "I want to showcase the integrity of the ingredient. I want the ingredient to be the star."

Yuzu-marinated Beet and Goat Cheese Salad

Yuzu-marinated Beet and Goat Cheese Salad

with Wild Arugula, Frisée, and Pistachio Vinaigrette

From Chad Starling of Aria

4 servings

BEETS

1 lb. baby red beets (peel on, stems removed)
1 lb. baby golden beets (peel on, stems removed)
1 lb. baby candy stripe beets (peel on, stems removed)
1/2 c. grapeseed or olive oil
1/2 c. water
Pinch of salt
3 cloves garlic, smashed
2 shallots, halved

BEET MARINADE

1 c. yuzu
1/2 c. sherry vinegar
1 1/2 c. sugar
2 c. water
1 cinnamon stick
1 tbsp. caraway seeds

Preheat oven to 375°F. Roast beets, covered, in roasting pan with oil, water, salt, garlic, and shallots for 40–50 minutes, or until tender. Remove beets from pan and let cool. Peel beets and leave whole or halve, depending on your preference. Bring marinade to a simmer, pour over beets, and chill.

VINAIGRETTE

2 c. pistachios, toasted and chopped
2 c. lime juice
2 tbsp. garlic, minced
2 tbsp. red chili (Fresno or jalapeño), minced 2 tbsp. shallot, minced
1 to 1 1/2 cups grape seed or olive oil
1 tsp. Thai fish sauce
Salt, to taste

Combine all ingredients. Reserve.

SALAD

4 oz. Capriole (or other good-quality) goat cheese
1 lb. Nichols Farm arugula and frisée

Slice a few ounces of Capriole goat cheese and put on serving platter. Place marinated beets around cheese. Toss Nichols Farm arugula and frisée with vinaigrette and place on top of cheese. Garnish with more cheese and vinaigrette.

Ricotta Gnocchi
with Michigan Morels, Fava Beans, Spinach, and Parmesan

From Chad Starling of Aria

4 servings

GNOCCHI

- 1 lb. fresh ricotta cheese
- 1 farm egg, beaten
- 1/2 cup Parmigiano-Reggiano cheese, grated
- Salt and pepper, to taste
- 1 tbsp. chives, minced
- 2/3 cup all-purpose flour, plus extra for rolling

Mix together ricotta and beaten egg. Add Parmigiano-Reggiano cheese, salt, pepper, and chives. Then slowly add flour to obtain the right consistency. Let rest for 5 minutes. Sprinkle work surface liberally with flour so dough does not stick. Scoop about a tennis-ball-sized piece of dough with your hands and start rolling it into a long cylinder on your work surface, about 3/4 in. thick. Once the cylinder is even and completely rolled out, cut into 1-in. dumplings. Place on a floured sheet pan until ready to cook. Bring water to a simmer, not a boil, and add gnocchi. Remove gnocchi when they float and put into an oiled pan to cool.

REMAINING INGREDIENTS

- 1 tbsp. olive oil
- 18–20 medium-sized morel mushrooms, cleaned, cut in half
- 1 tbsp. butter
- 1 tbsp. shallot, minced
- 1 tbsp. garlic, minced
- 2 handfuls raw farm spinach, stems trimmed
- 1 lb. fava beans, shucked, blanched, and peeled
- Salt and pepper, to taste
- 1/2 c. vegetable or chicken stock
- 1/4 c. Parmigiano-Reggiano cheese, grated
- 1 tbsp. chives
- 1 tbsp. basil

In a large sauté pan, heat olive oil and add about 25 or 30 gnocchi. Sauté about 1 minute until gnocchi turn golden brown. Add morels and sauté for 30 seconds before adding butter, shallots, and garlic. Sauté just until butter is slightly browned, then add spinach, fava beans, salt, and pepper. Sauté for another 15–20 seconds and add stock, cheese, chives, and basil. Adjust seasoning, if necessary. Garnish with more cheese, chives, and basil.

Butter-poached Peekytoe Crab

with Cueball Squash, Tempura-fried Squash Blossom, and Fava Bean-Thai Basil Puree

From Chad Starling of Aria

4 servings

CUEBALL SQUASH

4 cueball squash
1 tbsp. olive oil
Salt and pepper, to taste

Wash and cut squash straight down the middle and scoop out seeds. Leave some flesh intact, but scoop out enough of the seeds to form a cup for the crab. Brush squash with olive oil and season with salt and pepper. Place squash on hot grill or roast in a 400°F oven until tender but still firm.

PEEKYTOE CRAB

1 lb. peekytoe crab (or jumbo lump blue crab)
1/4 lb. butter
1 tbsp. shallot, minced
1 tsp. garlic, minced
Salt and pepper, to taste
1 lemon, juiced
1 tablespoon Thai basil, cut into ribbons

In saucepan over medium heat, fold together crab, butter, shallot, garlic, salt and pepper, and lemon juice. When hot, fold in Thai basil and season to taste.

FAVA PUREE

1/4–1/2 c. vegetable or chicken stock, warm
1/4 lb. fava beans, blanched and peeled
Salt and pepper, to taste
1 lemon, juiced
1/2 bunch Thai basil

In blender, blend stock with fava beans, salt and pepper, lemon juice, and Thai basil. Strain puree through a fine-mesh strainer.

TEMPURA SQUASH

2 c. cake flour
1/2 c. cornstarch
1/2 tsp. baking soda
1/2 tsp. salt
Soda water, cold
4 squash blossoms
Grated lemon zest, from one lemon
Oil for frying

Mix dry ingredients together. Slowly mix in soda water with chopsticks until a pancake-batter consistency forms. Dredge blossoms in tempura batter and deep-fry until golden at 350°F. Spoon some fava puree onto plate. Place two squash cups on puree and fill with crab mixture. Garnish with a squash blossom and grated lemon zest.

Frontera Grill, Topolobampo, and XOCO

Chef Rick Bayless

Mick Klug

Rick Bayless, one of the country's most celebrated chefs, was also one of the first in Chicago to begin looking for his ingredients close to home. But he came of age at a time when there was a great cultural identity crisis surrounding locally grown foods.

Bayless, who grew up in Oklahoma City, remembers his Depression-era parents and grandparents planting, canning, and preserving.

"They were always planting a garden, always celebrating the different things that were in season," he says.

At the same time, though, there was a different kind of "green revolution" going on, in which most everything was grown with insecticides and fertilizers. Frozen foods became modern, must-have items.

He recalled his jam-making grandmother beaming with pride when she bought a big chest freezer.

"She was so incredibly proud of this deep freeze," he says. "She did fill it with some of her own stuff. But she was really happy when people could see her pull out the BirdsEye peas. She was conflicted."

Bayless sided more with the hippies who were building compost piles and cultivating sourdough starters to bake bread. It's a philosophy he carried with him when he opened his first Chicago restaurant—Frontera Grill—in 1987.

There was little infrastructure for local food in Chicago at the time, but Bayless thought locally sourced foods might help set him apart. (In fact, many high-end restaurants at the time promoted their exotic ingredients from far away, he says.) So, he went to area farm stands in search of strawberries—his first local ingredient.

That's when Bayless first got to know farmer Mick Klug, who would deliver strawberries to Frontera.

"We made a pact at that time that the only strawberries on our menu would be locally grown strawberries," Bayless says. "It took us a long time and a huge amount of dedication to get to the place where we could actually have a significant amount of local stuff on the menu. For the last ten years now, during the height of the season, we're 90 percent all-local ingredients."

With Bayless' three incredibly popular Chicago restaurants—Frontera Grill, Topolobampo, and XOCO—maintaining good relationships with farmers has been essential when ordering such massive quantities.

"They are our partners," he says. "We consider them partners in the restaurant."

As further evidence of his commitment to local farmers, Bayless formed the Frontera Farmer Foundation, which began as a no-interest loan program for growers to buy equipment to increase production. The program eventually became a foundation, which has since given away three-quarters of a million dollars in small grants to food producers.

"We have really helped jump-start the great local agriculture and put it to a level that people can make a living at it," he says.

Bayless first met Klug about nineteen years ago at the farmers' market in Lincoln Park. He now buys pound after pound of raspberries, black raspberries, blackberries, peaches, gooseberries, pluots, apples, pears, and asparagus from Klug.

Bayless was Klug's first chef customer. As Bayless started buying more produce, "that's when we realized there was a market to cater to restaurants," Klug says.

Klug, who was born and raised on the farm in south St. Joseph, Michigan, went through a phase after high school in which he didn't know if farming was for him.

"Farming is a struggle," he says. "It's seven twenty-fours. It's pretty intense."

But other factors won out: "The flexibility of being your own boss, your own worker, and working with the land," he says. "It's very rewarding when you plant something and it grows."

Klug now owns 40 acres and rents an additional 80 acres of land. Over the years, he has adjusted his crops a bit to meet the needs of chefs.

"We have upped our acreage in asparagus; that is getting to be a big seller," Klug says. "We're always planting more Honeycrisp apples. We're always looking for more varieties of peaches to try. We're planting more Asian pears."

It has been a bit surreal over the years to work so closely with such a well-known chef, Klug says. "There's people taking our pictures with him," he says. "He has really done well for himself. He's true blue. What he does is what he believes in."

Tartaletas Rústica de Manzana
con Cajeta y Salsa de Moras
(Rustic *Cajeta* Apple Tarts
with Berry "Salsa")

From Rick Bayless

The easy, foolproof pastry for these rustic tarts was inspired by a recipe from Rose Levy Beranbaum's remarkable The Pie and Pastry Bible.

Makes 6 individual tarts

1 1/3 c. (6 oz.) all-purpose flour
1/8 tsp. baking powder
1/8 tsp. salt
6 oz. (3/4 c.) unsalted butter, cold, cut into small pieces
1 3-oz. package cream cheese, cold, cut into small pieces
1 1/2 tsp. cider vinegar
1 1/2 tbsp. ice water
5 medium (about 2 lb. total) firm cooking apples, such as Gala or Granny Smith
1 tsp. lime or lemon zest, finely chopped
1 c. *cajeta*, store-bought or homemade
2 c. berries, such as raspberries, blackberries, or hulled, sliced strawberries (defrosted quick-frozen berries will work)
1–2 tbsp. sugar, to taste
3/4 c. homemade *crema*, crème fraîche, or sour cream thinned with a little milk (optional)

In a food processor, combine flour, baking powder, and salt. Pulse to mix thoroughly. Add 4 oz. (1/2 c.) of butter and all the cream cheese, then pulse 5 or 6 times until the mixture looks like coarse crumbs. Drizzle the vinegar and ice water over the dough, and pulse 3 times to bring the mixture together into rough clumps. Turn out onto your work surface, divide into 6 parts, and roll each into a ball. Place the balls on a plate, cover with plastic wrap, and refrigerate for about 45 minutes.

Peel and core the apples, then cut them into 1/2-in. cubes. You should have about 6 c.

In a large (12-in.) heavy skillet (preferably nonstick), heat the remaining 2 oz. (1/4 c.) of butter over medium-high heat. Add the apples and stir nearly constantly as they cook, first releasing their juice, then softening and browning as the juice evaporates, about 8–10 minutes. When the apples are soft (if you've chosen the firm-cooking apples, they won't be falling apart) and browned, add 1/2 tsp. of the lime or lemon zest and 1/4 c. of the *cajeta*. Stir for a minute or two, then remove from the heat. Scoop the apple mixture onto a baking sheet to cool to room temperature, about 15 minutes.

While the apples are cooling, roll out each ball of dough into a 6-in. round on a lightly floured work surface. Transfer the pastry rounds to a parchment-covered or lightly oiled baking sheet, leaving about 2 in. between the rounds. If the apples haven't cooled to room temperature by this point, cover the pastry rounds with plastic wrap and refrigerate.

Spoon 1/3 c. of the filling onto the center of each pastry round, leaving a 1 1/2-in. border all around. Carefully fold the dough edges up over the filling toward the center, gently pleating the dough as necessary. If time allows, place the baking sheet in the freezer for about 20 minutes.

Heat the oven to 400°F. Bake the tarts until richly golden and crispy, about 20–25 minutes. Remove from the oven and drizzle a generous 1/2 tbsp. of the remaining *cajeta* into the center of each tart. Cool on a wire rack.

In a small bowl, mix the berries with the remaining 1/4 tsp. of lime or lemon zest and the sugar. Mash the mixture slightly to crush some of the berries. Let the mixture stand a few minutes to meld the flavors.

Serve the tarts warm with a spoonful or two of the optional crema or sour cream, the berry "salsa," and a little drizzle of the remaining *cajeta*.

Working ahead: Both the dough and filling can be made 3 days ahead if kept well-covered and refrigerated. Formed tarts can be held for 6 hours or so in the refrigerator (skip the freezing step, instead simply cover them with plastic and refrigerate). These tarts are best served within 3 or 4 hours of their baking. Rewarming cool tarts gives them renewed life.

Cazuela de Frutas Empolvoronadas (Skillet Fruit Crisp)

From Rick Bayless

Serves 6

4 oz. (1 stick, 8 tbsp.) softened butter, preferably unsalted (divided)

2 lb. nectarines or peaches, peeled, pitted, and cut into 1/2-in. slices (see note for other fruit options)

1/2 c. plus 2 tbsp. white sugar (divided)

2/3 c. flour, preferably whole wheat or whole-grain spelt flour

1/4 c. brown sugar

1/2 tsp. ground cinnamon, preferably Mexican *canela*

1/2 tsp. salt

3/4 c. (3 oz.) *pepitas* (pumpkin seeds), toasted, or any toasted, coarsely chopped nuts

Preheat the oven to 400°F. Set a medium (10-in.) skillet with ovenproof handle over medium heat and add 2 tbsp. of the butter. When it begins to brown, add the fruit. Sprinkle with 2 tbsp. of the white sugar. Cook, stirring regularly, until the fruit is soft, most of the juice it has exuded has evaporated, about 10 minutes.

While the fruit is cooking, stir together the flour, the remaining 1/2 c. white sugar, the brown sugar, cinnamon, and salt (use only 1/4 tsp. salt if you have salted the *pepitas*) in a medium-size bowl. Add remaining 6 tbsp. of the butter, working it in with a wooden spoon until a homogenous mixture is formed (you can do this step with a mixer or food processor).

With a spoon, stir in the *pepitas* (or other nuts). Crumble this streusel topping evenly over the cooked fruit mixture. Slide the skillet into the oven and cook for 10–15 minutes, until the topping is crispy. Serve warm or at room temperature.

Variations: You can replace the apples or pears. If you'd like to make the crisp with plums (pitted, not peeled), combine 1 lb. plums with 1 lb. of apples or pears for body, because the plums' juiciness causes them to disintegrate in the cooking. Ditto for berries: Use 1 1/2 lb. of apples or pears along with 1/2 lb. of berries.

The Dining Room at Kendall College

Chef Benjamin Browning

Simply Wisconsin

The day Benjamin Browning ran out of tomatoes changed his life as a chef.

Browning, who grew up in the small farming community of Holland, Michigan, had been working his way up through the ranks of the food industry since he was fourteen years old. But he hadn't thought much about local produce until the day he ran out of tomatoes while working as a chef at Butch's Dry Dock in his hometown.

"There was a farmers' market three blocks away," Browning says. "And I knew where I should go. I went to the farmers' market and got the best tomatoes I'd ever had. It just opened my eyes to a whole new way of doing things."

Now Browning runs the Dining Room at Kendall College, one of the country's top culinary schools. He teaches a course in fine dining there and tries to impress upon his students the value of using locally grown ingredients.

"It's amazing how little they do know about it, how eye-opening it is," Browning says. "Once they get the concept and once they taste a real carrot, it's the same eye-opening experience I had.

"One of my students tried a black walnut for the first time yesterday. I told her, 'These black walnuts are $36 per pound. But when you taste it, you realize why it's so special and why they're so expensive.'"

Kendall College has been a leader in training future chefs about environmentally sound practices. The school offers a class on sustainability and environmental science. All of the teaching kitchens have compost and recycling bins.

Browning also works with students to think about getting the most out of their food dollars. Since fresh, local ingredients are so flavorful, you don't need to use as much of them in a dish as you would of produce shipped from far away, he says. Plus, there's less waste with locally sourced foods.

"When things are fresh, they stay fresh a lot longer," he says.

But he cautions the up-and-coming chefs about making a big deal about cooking with local ingredients. There's no need to take out a billboard to advertise it, he says.

"It speaks for itself," Browning says. "If you're doing it properly, you don't need to say anything about it. Cooking wholesome food is exactly what we should be doing. This isn't a trend. Sustainability, eating local, is a way of life. It's the way it's always been done."

Browning came to Chicago and started working at MK. The high-end restaurant uses local ingredients and also served as a drop-off point for a Wisconsin farm cooperative CSA. That's how Browning got to know Deb Hanson, who now runs Simply Wisconsin, a farming collective.

"He was the first restaurant customer we had," Hanson says of Browning, who buys meat, nuts, parsnips, watercress, and other produce from Simply Wisconsin. "What we do is work with growers who don't do their own marketing. I leave the growing to the farmers."

Hanson works with about forty different organic farmers in Wisconsin who sell produce, cheese, meat, eggs, and preserves. The farmers pay her to handle all of their marketing and to make restaurant deliveries. Simply Wisconsin also runs a 1,200-member CSA.

"We set the price we think will be competitive and fair to the consumer and chefs, and we work backward and set our farm prices from that," Hanson says. "You have to be able to offer things at an affordable price."

Hanson grew up in Oregon, Wisconsin, and was raised on a farm until she was six. Her parents were farmers and her paternal grandfather was a farmer and an agriculture teacher.

"We spent summers on his farm, helping with lambing and the garden and helping him with beekeeping," she says. "He's probably the one person who taught all of my entire family the value of not offending Mother Nature, not taking for granted what you've been given.

"That's what we try to do. To pass that along to people. Don't take your food for granted."

Over the years, Hanson has watched the farms disappear from the area in which she grew up. And she becomes melancholy, watching the average age of farmers climb.

"It's really sad," she says. "They've been forced to sell to developers to make way for new roads."

She's encouraged, though, by her own daughters' interest in local foods.

"My fifteen-year-old came with us to all the farmers' markets last year," she says. "And my youngest daughter is our organic advocate. She also comes and helps with box pack-up for the CSA."

Applewood-grilled Asparagus Soup

Applewood-grilled Asparagus Soup

From Benjamin Browning of Kendall College

Serves 4

- 10 oz. asparagus (no woody ends)
- 1 tbsp. grapeseed oil
- 1 tsp. kosher salt, divided
- 1/4 oz. sorrel
- 10 oz. herb broth (recipe follows)
- 1 oz. washed spinach
- 1/4 tsp. black peppercorns

Prepare the grill by turning it to high and cover one side with a cookie sheet. Soak 4 oz. applewood chips in water for 30 minutes, remove water, and wrap in a 4x6-in. foil pouch. Punch many holes in the pouch. Place the pouch under the hottest grates of a very hot grill.

Wash and trim the asparagus, saving the woody ends for the herb broth and the tips for the garnish. Toss asparagus with oil and salt. When the chips begin to smoke, grill the asparagus, covered with a small cookie sheet, until lightly cooked and slightly browned (about 3–5 minutes). Combine the remaining ingredients in a blender and puree until smooth, taste to adjust seasoning, and strain through a fine strainer.

Sorrel Crackers

From Benjamin Browning of Kendall College

- 2 c. unbleached all-purpose flour
- 3 tbsp. superfine baker's sugar
- 2 tsp. kosher salt
- 2 oz. unsalted butter, melted
- 6 oz. white wine vinegar
- 7 oz. water
- 1 tsp. sorrel, minced
- 2 tsp. Hawaiian red salt

Mix together the dry ingredients. Add in the wet ingredients with the butter last. Mix just to combine, with no lumps It should be like pancake batter. Refrigerate batter, covered, for 1 hour.

Preheat oven to 325°F. Mix the sorrel into the batter. Spread batter very thinly on a silicone baking mat. Score to desired size, such as 2x6 in., sprinkle with salt. Bake for 10 minutes and turn down to 275°F for 5 minutes until the crackers are completely golden. Let cool on mat.

Herb Broth

From Benjamin Browning of Kendall College

Makes 1 gallon

- 1 tbsp. grapeseed oil
- 1 lb. yellow onion, julienned
- 8 oz. asparagus trimmings, woody ends included
- 8 oz. spring onion, halved
- 2 whole cloves garlic
- 1/2 fennel bulb, julienned
- 1/2 leek, julienned
- 6 oz. chardonnay
- 1 gal. water
- 10 sprigs thyme
- 2 fresh bay leaves
- 2 sprigs fresh rosemary
- 1 bunch Italian parsley
- 5 sprigs fresh savory
- 2 sprigs tarragon
- 3/4 oz. lovage

Lightly sweat the vegetables (not the herbs) in the oil until translucent. Deglaze the pan with chardonnay, reduce by half. Add in the water and simmer for 1 hour. Tear the herbs with your hands and stir them into the stock. Simmer 10 more minutes. Let the broth cool at room temperature for 30 minutes. Strain.

To finish the soup, sear the 2 oz. of morels and 2 oz. of asparagus tips in a very hot skillet with a splash of grapeseed oil, salt, and pepper. Drain on paper towels.

In a small saucepan, warm the asparagus and mushrooms with slivered spring onions, argan oil, salt, and pepper. Pour the soup into the bowl, place the cracker on top, and stack the sautéed garnish on top of the cracker.

Wood-roasted Chicken

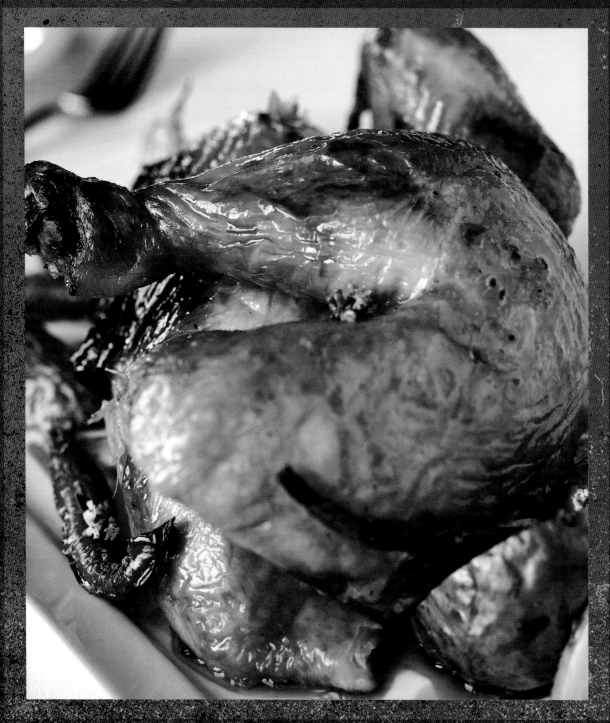

Wood-roasted Chicken
with Market Vegetables and Jus Roti

From Benjamin Browning of Kendall College

Serves 4

- 2 free-range chickens
- 4 qt. lavender citrus brine (recipe follows)
- 8 oz. carrot, halved
- 12 oz. fennel bulb, quartered
- 8 oz. fingerling potatoes, halved
- 8 oz. spring onion bulb
- 12 cloves garlic
- 4 sprig fresh savory
- 2 oz. grapeseed oil
- 4 tsp. kosher salt
- 1 tsp. ground black peppercorns
- 1 tbsp. white wine vinegar
- 1 tbsp. sorrel, small dice
- 1 tbsp. fresh chives, minced
- 2 oz. chicken sauce (recipe follows)

Lavender Citrus Brine

From Benjamin Browning of Kendall College

- 2 tbsp. whole coriander seeds
- 2 1/2 gal. water
- 8 oz. kosher salt
- 8 oz. sugar
- 3 tbsp. lavender
- zest of 2 lemons
- zest of 1 orange
- 5 crushed bay leaves

Lightly toast the coriander seeds until lightly fragrant, but not smoking. Crack the seeds with a rolling pin.

Bring half the water to a simmer, add in the salt, sugar, lavender, citrus zest, coriander seeds, and bay leaves. Let steep at room temperature for 30 minutes. Remove from heat and add in the remaining water in the form of Ice by weight.

Chicken Sauce

- 2 1/2 lb. roasted chicken wings
- 2 oz. chicken fat
- 1 lb. carrots, small dice
- 1 lb. yellow onion, small dice
- 1/2 celery stalk, small dice
- 1/2 tsp. cracked black peppercorns
- 2 fresh bay leaves
- 1/2 oz. thyme
- 1 gal. chicken stock (preferably homemade, recipe follows)
- 1 bottle chardonnay wine

Roast the chicken wings until well caramelized on a roasting pan in a 375°F oven (reserve roasted wings and use the rendered fat to caramelize the vegetables). In a large pot, lightly caramelize the vegetables in the rendered chicken fat. Deglaze with the white wine, reduce until almost dry. Add in the roasted chicken wings, thyme, and chicken stock, bring to a simmer. Reduce by half, strain through a fine strainer. Adjust seasoning. Cool, cover, and refrigerate.

To finish the dish, submerge the whole chickens in brine overnight, refrigerated. Remove chickens from the brine. Pat them dry, inside and out, lightly salt the skin, truss, and place on a roasting rack. Roast in a wood-fired oven at 325°F or in a conventional oven at 350°F until the internal temperature reaches 165°F. Let rest at room temperature before serving.

Add the pan drippings to the roasted vegetables. Toss them with the garlic and savory, along with the oil, salt, and pepper. Roast the vegetables in the 350°F oven until tender. To serve, lay a bed of vegetables on each plate and place a split breast and leg on each one. Serve with the roasted chicken sauce.

Nacional 27

Mixologist Adam Seger
Harvest Moon Organics

Adam Seger wants to make the concept of "farm-to-bar" as well-known and accepted as "farm-to-table."

The mixologist from Nacional 27 in River North has gone beyond simply picking fresh produce from area farmers' markets for his inventive cocktails. He collaborated with Harvest Moon Organics to plant his own plot of drink-ready produce and has planted a rooftop herb garden atop his downtown office (with soil trucked in from Harvest Moon) to add further local zest to his mojitos, caipirinhas, and other cocktails.

"I see the cocktail world really kind of following the culinary world," Seger says. "With the mixology movement really starting to explode in the last three to four years, I see the same thing happening with cocktails."

For the past several years, Seger had been visiting Chicago-area farmers' markets in search of top-notch produce for his Nacional 27 cocktails. And then a few summers ago, "I found the most absolutely stunning rhubarb I've ever seen," Seger recalls. The rhubarb, he soon learned, came from Harvest Moon. He used it to create a Strawberry-Rhubarb-Basil-Balsamic Mojito that *GQ* magazine proclaimed one of the twenty best cocktails in America in 2008.

He sat down with the farmers from Harvest Moon, poring over an heirloom seed catalog. They let him choose whatever seeds he liked and set aside a tennis-court-sized garden plot for him.

"Then, we wrote a cocktail plan based on that," Seger says.

Last year, all of the recipients of Harvest Moon's CSA boxes started receiving a cocktail recipe from Seger each week.

"It's been a really cool process," he says. "Each year, we've been figuring out what to do to make it more sustainable."

It's little surprise Seger takes his cocktails so seriously. He approaches them with chef's perspective, having spent time working at Napa Valley's famed French Laundry and at Chicago's highly regarded Tru, among others.

"I've loved to cook really since I was a little kid," Seger says. "I've got a really strong culinary background."

Seger also recently created and bottled his own liqueur called Hum. The ruby-colored, 70-proof spirit infuses organic rum with hibiscus, ginger, green cardamom, and kaffir lime. He gives herbs from his rooftop garden as a thank-you to bartenders around Chicago who use Hum.

Bob Borchardt of Harvest Moon and his wife, Jennifer, got into farming in a roundabout sort of way. For two decades, Bob worked in food-service operations. Then, he got out of that business and started a video company geared toward the food, wine, and spirit industry. (It was on one of those video shoots that he first meet Seger.)

About five years ago, he went to Argentina to shoot a video for a wine company. Jennifer Borchardt saw the footage from an organic farm while her husband was editing film and said, "That looks pretty cool. We should do that someday," Bob Borchardt says. So, they did.

Borchardt had won contests for his garden over the years, but, "I never really thought I was going to do this," he says.

Jennifer Borchardt started interning on farms and taking classes in organic farming.

They now farm about 30 acres in Viroqua, Wisconsin, and have a fast-growing CSA membership and restaurant client list. They consider themselves lucky to have found farmland in a tremendously fertile valley that used to be home to a cow pasture.

"We've been in the food business, but creating food like the way we're doing it is just something completely different," Bob Borchardt says. "It's really gratifying to do what we do, but it's really hard work. We're constantly learning."

The Borchardts hosted a big party on the farm for their CSA members, with dining tables out in the field. Bob Borchardt's brother, a professional chef, did the cooking.

"Watching people consume the food was just unbelievable," he says. "It just validated (that) we knew as a family we were doing the right thing.

"Our goal is to simply be some part of changing how the food world works. We're just trying to do what we can to bring this thing back to somewhat of a local thing."

Strawberry-Rhubarb-Basil-Balsamic Mojito

From Adam Seger of Nacional 27, originally published in the August 2008 issue of "GQ" magazine as one of the twenty best cocktails in America

Serves 1

3 medium-sized strawberries, sliced
1 tbsp. sliced rhubarb that has been softened in a hot pan with 2 tsp. brown sugar
1/2 lime, quartered, bitter white pith removed
Loosely packed fresh basil, enough to fill one quarter of the glass
1 1/2 oz. 10 Cane Rum
Soda water
Best-quality balsamic vinegar

Muddle all ingredients in a sturdy pint glass until juicy and aromatic. Add rum. Fill glass with ice and a splash of soda. Stir, add another splash of soda.

Top with a dash of the best balsamic vinegar you can afford. Garnish with a fresh strawberry, a basil sprig, a sugar cane stick, and a rhubarb stir stick.

Summer Hummin'

From Adam Seger of Nacional 27

Serves 1

1 1/2 oz. Hum
Ginger beer
Harvest Moon organic cucumber
Harvest Moon organic basil

Pour Hum (herbal-infused rum) in a highball glass. Fill with ice and top with ginger beer. Garnish with a long slice of cucumber and sprigs of basil.

Snap-pea-irinha

From Adam Seger of Nacional 27

Serves 1

1 lime, cut in eighths, bitter white center pith removed
1/2 c. spring snap peas
1 oz. simple syrup (equal parts sugar and water, simmered until sugar dissolves, and cooled)
1 1/2 oz. gin
Fresh-cracked pepper

Muddle lime and peas in a heavy rocks glass until limes are juicy and peas are crushed. Add simple syrup and gin (North Shore Distillery for a local Chicago gin, Hendrick's for a cucumbery gin, CapRock for organic, or Bombay Sapphire for a classic). Fill with ice (preferably crushed) and stir. Finish with fresh-cracked pepper.

Gazpacho and Tonic

From Adam Seger of Nacional 27

Serves 1

2 cucumbers, sliced
1 melon of choice, sliced
2 bulbs fennel, sliced
1 bottle Death's Door gin

Cover equal parts sliced cucumbers, melons, and fennel with Death's Door gin. Infuse refrigerated in a glass jar overnight or up to 2 weeks.

1/2 lime, quartered, bitter white center pith discarded
1 1/2 oz. CapRock gin
Splash of tonic

Fill a 12-oz. rocks glass halfway with the infused produce. Add the lime pieces. Muddle until the melons and cucumbers are juicy and the fennel is slightly smashed. Add gin. Fill with ice, top with tonic.

Heirloom Tomato Mojitonico

From Adam Seger of Nacional 27

Serves 1

Salt and fresh-cracked peppercorns
3 oz. tomatoes, chopped
2 oz. mixed herbs (basil, dill, thyme, tarragon, chives
—whole leaves)
1/2 lime, quartered
1 1/2 oz. gin, preferably North Shore Distillery No. 6
Tonic

Rim a 16-oz. pint glass with salt and fresh-cracked pepper. Muddle tomatoes, herbs, and limes in the glass until the mixture is half juice, half solids. Fill glass with ice. Add gin, fill with tonic.

Heirloom Tomato Mojito

From Adam Seger of Nacional 27

Serves 1

1/2 lime, quartered
1/4 medium-sized green tomato, quartered
1/4 medium-sized heirloom tomato, quartered
12 basil leaves
Pinch kosher salt
3 pinches fresh black pepper
1 1/2 oz. Gran Centenario Plata tequila
Tonic water
Splash of aged balsamic vinegar
Basil-sprig garnish

Combine the lime, tomatoes, basil, salt, and pepper in empty pint glass. Muddle and add ice. Pour in tequila and top with tonic water and a splash of balsamic vinegar. Garnish with basil sprig.

Prairie Grass Café and Prairie Fire

Chefs Sarah Stegner and George Bumbaris
River Valley Ranch and Kitchens

Back in 1977, Eric Rose's father was a bit shorthanded on the family mushroom farm and asked his son to pitch in.

"I've been trying to get out ever since," he says with a laugh.

In that time, he has helped turn Burlington, Wisconsin-based River Valley Ranch and Kitchens into a farmers' market favorite and a regular provider of mushrooms to chefs around Chicago.

Rose and his family produce some 7,000 pounds of criminis, portabellas, shitakes, and oyster mushrooms each week without using chemicals, pesticides, or growth enhancers.

Their biggest sellers, the criminis, are grown as part of a seventy-day process that begins with compost. After about twenty days outside, the compost is taken indoors for pasteurization and conditioning. Then each 35-ton batch of the special compost is inoculated with about 800 pounds of mushroom spawn. If all goes well, the spawn begins growing in the compost and continues for about twenty days. After that time, temperature, humidity, ventilation, and carbon dioxide levels in the mushroom house are changed to shock the plants into fruiting. (Given the complicated growing process, it continues to astound Rose every time he seems a mushroom growing wild in nature.)

"They will form into a pinhead, which, eventually, if conditions are right, will mature," Rose says.

River Valley Ranch also produces a line of jarred salsas, dips, and pickled vegetables. And the kitchen is at work on some ready-to-eat mushroom patties.

Rose's dad handled the business side of the mushroom business, so Rose learned the ins and outs of growing from a retired mushroom grower. About eight months after he took over the farm, he says he got a little cocky and thought he had the art and science all figured out.

"I got humbled early on," Rose says. "I kind of fell flat on my face. If I make a mistake in week one, I won't see the results of that until week seven. It's a lot of guess and test."

Rose has struggled over the years as more varieties of mushrooms have flooded the market. When he started selling them, few people had even heard of those big, beefy portobellos. Now, they're everywhere. And Rose is concerned about high-production growers who use chemicals or other means to increase volume or create more perfect-looking mushrooms.

"For me, it's more than growing this commodity that turns into dollars," Rose says. "We're growing food here. It's not just mushrooms I make money with, it's food and it's life. And producing that carries a responsibility."

Chefs Sarah Stegner and George Bumbaris have worked together for more than a quarter century, starting at Chicago's Ritz-Carlton. The two now run Prairie Grass Cafe in Northbrook, Illinois, as well as the recently opened Prairie Fire in Chicago's West Loop.

All along, they've had a strong commitment to working with locally grown ingredients.

"We basically started it with an idea of how to increase the quality of what goes on my tables at the restaurant," Stegner says. "I just kept coming across the same thing—that what tastes the best is what's out of the ground and what's in season."

Stegner was one of the founding members of the Green City Market, a move borne in part out of wanting to make it easier for chefs to connect with local growers.

"It was difficult to source if you weren't hooked into a particular farm," Stegner says. "It was hard to find them. There was no distribution system."

Stegner and Bumbaris buy large amounts of produce from local farmers, including mushrooms from River Valley for stock, sautés, strudels, and other dishes.

"We use a ton of mushrooms from those guys," Bumbaris says.

Bumbaris, who was born in the former Czechoslovakia, grew up eating an in-season diet. He's also a gardener, so "I kind of know what a tomato should taste like," he says.

As the executive chef of the Ritz-Carlton, he began finding locally grown ingredients for the hotel early on, simply because the products are top-notch.

"Number one is the quality of the product, and the rest of it just makes sense after that," Bumbaris says.

Some chefs criticize others for simply putting local foods on the menu to drive business. There's no room for criticism, Stegner says. Whatever the motive, it's a smart move to support area growers.

"You should never shake your finger at somebody who is trying to break into the local food scene," she says. "You have to think about what your restaurant can afford, what makes sense. One restaurant, buying one item, if they go through enough of it, can make an impact on that farmer's income."

For the past couple of seasons, Stegner has installed a webcam in the garden at her home so diners can check out the progress.

"We had a garden, and my grandfather had a garden in his backyard," she says. "I think it makes a difference if you can connect and you know what it takes to grow the product."

Mushroom Asparagus Ragout

From Sarah Stegner and George Bumbaris
of Prairie Grass Café

Serves 4

1 c. white button mushrooms, stems removed and cut
  into eighths
1 c. portobello mushrooms, stems removed and undersides
  of the mushrooms scraped clean
2 tbsp. olive oil
Salt
Fresh-ground black pepper
1/4 c. shallots, minced
1/2 c. mushroom or chicken stock
2 tbsp. butter
2 tbsp. flat leaf parsley, chopped
2 tbsp. basil leaves, thinly sliced
8 thick stalks of asparagus, peeled
1/8 c. Pleasant Ridge Reserve cheese shavings

In a large skillet over medium-high heat, sauté the mushrooms in
olive oil. Season with salt and pepper. Cook the mushrooms until
any juices have evaporated and they are golden brown. Add the
shallots and sauté until they are tender. If the pan looks dry, add a
bit more olive oil.

Add the mushroom (or chicken) stock. Lower the heat and simmer
until the stock is two-thirds reduced in volume. Add the butter and
stir until the butter is incorporated into the liquid. Taste and adjust
seasoning. Add the parsley and basil just before serving.

Cook the asparagus in boiling salted water for 2 minutes or until
tender. Remove from the pot of water and cut the asparagus into
2-in. pieces. Sauté in butter and add salt, if necessary. Spoon
the pieces of asparagus over the ragout. Sprinkle the ragout with
Pleasant Ridge Reserve cheese.

sola

Chef Carol Wallack

Werp Farms

Carol Wallack wanted to be a professional surfer when she grew up. She spent her early years in the water and on beaches in California and Hawaii. But once she realized that was a tough way to pay the bills, she discovered another passion.

"I kind of needed a job," Wallack says. "I liked food. And I needed a job."

Wallack started working at restaurants in Los Angeles, including the famed Spago, first in the front of the house, but she soon made her way to the kitchen. She knew from the start that fresh, local, seasonal foods would be her focus.

"I grew up in California," she says. "We're very conscious of weight and health. In Hawaii, I spent the majority of my lifetime in a bikini. I wear it because I look good in it and I'm healthy. You have to fuel your body with a good product."

Wallack's father used to take her to Chez Panisse, the temple of locally sourced ingredients.

"It was [Chez Panisse's chef] Alice Waters," she says. "She was a tremendous inspiration for me. And the desire to learn about this type of eating and eating well and fueling your body well. She really sparked an interest for my generation."

Wallack recalled a customer who asked for tomatoes in the dead of winter and insisted the restaurant should have them because the supermarket had them. Wallack held true to her seasonal principles.

"They're not local," she said. "They're not fresh. They're not good. It's wrong."

Wallack still has a home in Hawaii, but her sister convinced her to move to Chicago and start a restaurant. Wallack opened Deleece with her sister before opening her current restaurant, sola, in 2006 in Chicago's North Center neighborhood. Recently, Wallack moved sola downtown and opened the more budget-friendly ohana in its place. Ohana continues sola's farm-to-table mission.

"Chicago is a tremendous restaurant city," she says. "There's incredible competition and there's great camaraderie among the chefs and the farmers."

Wallack first heard about Werp Farms from Paul Virant of Vie. In a small-world coincidence, she discovered she went to the same high school and grew up in the same area of Los Angeles as farmer Tina Werp, though they didn't know each other.

"We both laughed about it," Wallack says.

Tina Werp met her husband, Mike, in the mid-1980s in northern Michigan, where he had been farming land that had been in his family since the turn of the twentieth century, when his great-grandfather emigrated from the former Czechoslovakia.

"These were hardscrabble farms," Tina Werp says. "You see those old pictures, man."

Mike Werp had been growing corn on the land since the mid-1970s, but the market for that crop began to take a nosedive. The Werps decided to diversify and began supplying produce for restaurants.

"We started with baby zucchini, French beans, and those little wild tomatoes," Tina Werp says. "It was perfect when we met. He had the land and a lot of knowledge about equipment and mechanics. And I'm the gardener, so I know how to look at a plant and know what's going on with it."

They now have eight greenhouses and farm about 10 acres of an 80-acre piece of land. The Werps are known for their microgreens and an assortment of heat-loving crops, including baby squash, squash blossoms, eggplant, and peppers.

"It's gorgeous soil," she says. "Northern Michigan has a lot of sand, but there's a couple of great spots. And we're in one of them."

The Werps work with about twenty chefs. They like to keep the number manageable so they can provided customized produce to each one. Making deliveries and seeing the Werp name on restaurant menus is very gratifying, Tina Werp says.

"It's fabulous," she says. "When you deliver to the restaurant and the chef opens the box and a couple of people come over and peek in and see what you've got, and they say, 'That's great,' or, 'That's beautiful.'"

The Werps are trying to make the farm as sustainable as possible. They plan to install geothermal heating for the greenhouses and also hope to put in a wind generator soon.

Two of the five children in the Werp's blended family plan to continue the family farm, she says, "even our fashionista who hated living out in the boondocks."

Tina and Mike Werp don't plan on retiring just yet. But Tina Werp says a little vacation might be nice.

"It's very, very hard work," she says. "With a restaurant, you have to be 100 percent. The produce has to be perfect, and you have to be consistent. If they put it on the menu, you'd better have it. They're counting on you."

Pineapple and Beet Salad

From Carol Wallack of sola

Serves 4

2 red Werp Farm beets
2 gold Werp Farm beets
4 Green Acres Farm radishes
Spicy greens from Werp Farm
1/2 pineapple, large dice
4 slices per salad Moonglo cheese from Prairie Fruits Farms,
   sliced or shaved

Preheat oven to 250°F. Wrap beets in foil and roast for about an hour (until soft but not mushy). Once cooled, dice beets into large chunks. Slice radishes. Clean greens.

DRESSING
1/4 shallot, minced
1/4 jalapeño skin, minced, no seeds or membrane
1/4 tsp. candied ginger
2 tbsp. yuzu juice
4 tbsp. rice wine vinegar
1/2 c. grapeseed oil

Whisk all dressing ingredients in a bowl. Combine all ingredients (including pineapple) in a serving bowl except dressing and cheese. Spoon dressing over the salad and toss. Arrange salad on four plates, garnish with shaved cheese.

Seared Wagyu Hanger Steak

From Carol Wallack of sola

Serves 4

  2 tsp. whole-grain mustard
  2 c. veal stock
  4 6-oz. Allen Brothers Wagyu hanger steaks
  Salt and pepper to taste
  1 bunch Werp Farms beet greens
  1 shallot, julienned
  4 farm eggs
  12 green asparagus spears
  Good-quality olive oil, for drizzling

STIR-FRIED JASMINE RICE
  1/4 c. jasmine rice
  1/2 c. water
  1 tsp. shallot, diced
  1 tsp. carrot, diced
  1 tsp. celery, diced
  1 tsp. garlic, minced
  1 tsp. ginger, minced
  1 tbsp. scallions, sliced
  1/8 tsp. sesame oil
  1 tbsp. soy sauce
  Salt and pepper, to taste

Put rice and water in a small pot on high heat and season with salt and pepper. Bring to a boil, then reduce heat to low and cover with a lid until rice is cooked, about 15 minutes.

In a hot sauté pan, sweat shallot, carrot, and celery for about 30 seconds. Add minced garlic and ginger and cook for another 30 seconds. Add the cooked rice and scallions. Finish with sesame oil and soy sauce.

Combine mustard and veal stock in a sauce pot. Reduce until sauce covers the back of a spoon.

Season the steaks with salt and pepper. Grill or sear until rare to medium rare. Let the steaks sit for 5 minutes before carving and serving.

Wash greens and remove tough vein/stem and rough-chop. In a sauté pan, sweat shallot and add greens. Add salt and pepper to season. Cook for 2–4 minutes, until greens are soft.

Drizzle oil over the asparagus and season with salt and pepper. Grill 4–6 minutes.

Poach 4 eggs, to soft.

To serve, place rice and beet greens on the plate, and fan the steak around the rice. Fan the asparagus, and gently crack the egg and place it over the rice.

summer

We suffered through the snowbanks.
We slogged through the slush and gray days,
dreaming of backyard barbecues of alfresco
dinners and picnics at the park.

Summer is here, and so are lava-red tomatoes
and corn sweeter than candy. Soak up the sun
while sipping blueberry-basil lemonade or nibbling
refreshing watermelon salad. Drink it all in;
this is what we have been waiting for.

Bleeding Heart Bakery

Chef Michelle Garcia

Growing Power

Utter the words "punk rock pastry" in Chicago and most everyone knows what you're talking about.

Pastry chef Michelle Garcia of Bleeding Heart Bakery has created a pastry empire with her edgy, organic, locally sourced cupcakes, cakes, and other treats.

Garcia grew up in Chicago and moved to California as a teenager. As a child, she began eating a vegetarian diet. (About 30 percent of the food at Bleeding Heart is vegan.)

"We grew up going to farmers' markets," she says, taking a break from the kitchen in her colorful bakery on Chicago's north side.

She started working in kitchens at sixteen but decided to get serious about the career a few years later by enrolling at Chicago's Kendall College for culinary school. "Everybody always says, 'You're a girl. You should do pastry,'" Garcia says. "But I fought it."

Soon, though, she had enrolled in Chicago's French Pastry School. She started a candy-making business before traveling to Amsterdam to work in a "crazy cake shop." It was her first experience doing big cakes and also an early introduction to locally sourced products in a bakery.

"They were really focused on using local farmers," Garcia says. "They had a farm down the street with one cow. They got all the milk from there."

After returning to the States, Garcia worked in San Francisco as a pastry chef for the Four Seasons and for Whole Foods.

"Everything in San Francisco was focused on local and organic," she says.

Garcia had always wanted her own bakery, so she moved back to Chicago and started making pastries out of a shared-use rental kitchen. Her treats became a farmers' market favorite, enabling her to open Bleeding Heart several years ago.

Garcia and her husband now run the original location, plus two additional shops. She also has a wholesale baking business.

She adjusts her pastries each season to enjoy the flavors of farm-fresh fruits.

"My rule is I'm not going to feed anybody something I'm not going to feed my kids," she says.

For several years, Garcia has purchased farm-fresh produce from Growing Power, an urban-agriculture program in Chicago.

"Urban agriculture is a legitimate economic development tool, but it's also necessary for the city," says Erika Allen, Growing Power's Chicago project manager. "To be food-secure, people need to know how to grow food."

Allen grew up on her family's farm outside of Milwaukee, Wisconsin. Her father began the Growing Power program there, and Allen decided to expand it to Chicago in 2002.

Growing Power began as a way to teach local residents about urban agriculture.

"We weren't planning on being big growers," Allen says. "But the demand for local, year-round food began to increase."

Now, Growing Power farms about two acres around several sites in Chicago, but they're working on acquiring more land from the city. The program sells produce to about fifteen restaurants, as well as at the Green City Market. Allen says she particularly enjoys working with Garcia.

"It's been amazing to watch her business grow," Allen says. "She's got a great deal of integrity. She donates her baked goods to events and nonprofits and sees that work as being connected to the work she does. I just have a ton of respect for her."

Growing Power picks up compost from Bleeding Heart to use on the farm. Garcia typically buys greens, tomatoes, and edible flowers, along with eggs, milk, and butter from Growing Power. Some of the ingredients come from the Growing Power farm in Wisconsin.

Dozens of young people work with Growing Power in after-school and summer programs. They help grow the produce, harvest it, and sell it at farmers' markets.

"We respond to the needs of the community," Allen says. "And one of the biggest needs continues to be youth and youth having constructive things to do. We give them life skills, job skills, and teach them where food comes from."

Chilam Balam

Chef Chuy Valencia
Three Sisters Garden

Tracey Vowell spent some seventeen fast-paced years working her way up in the Frontera Grill kitchen. One day, her boss, Rick Bayless, asked her to find as many local farmers as she could to provide produce for the restaurant.

This was years before farm-to-table cooking became common.

"I was set on a path of discovery and veered off it," Vowell joked. While visiting a group of farms in Wisconsin, she had an epiphany: "This is hard work. This is really hard work," she said. "But look at the freedom they have. Look at the lifestyle they have."

Vowell bought about 10 acres near Kankakee, Illinois, in April 2000 with partner Kathe Roybal, and Three Sisters Garden was born. (The name comes from the Native American tradition of growing corn, beans, and squash in the same mounds.) Their heirloom tomatoes, summer squash, dried beans, microgreens, pea shoots, and other produce appear on the menus of about twenty-five Chicago-area restaurants.

But one of Three Sisters' biggest successes has been with *huitlacoche*—a naturally occurring corn fungus that most farmers avoid like the plague. But Vowell and Roybal inoculate their corn through the silk, ear by ear, to encourage the corn to produce the mushroom-like huitlacoche.

Vowell recalled giving a farm tour a few years back in which she showed off the fungus, commonly known as "corn smut."

"We wanted to show it to them," she says. "The stuff has a certain amount of shock value you can't ignore. One woman in the group was so horrified, it was unbelievable to watch her. This woman was going to be sick, and we were so proud."

But huitlacoche is prized by chefs for the dark, earthy sweetness it brings to sauces and fillings.

Chuy Valencia, the chef-owner of Chicago's hipster nuevo-Mexican restaurant, Chilam Balam, buys plenty of it from Three Sisters.

"Her huitlacoche is off the hook," Valencia says. "We use it in a bunch of stuff. We make it into sauce. We use it as filling. You can make quesadillas with it. You can fill crispy tacos with it. You can make mole with it. They're just very interesting vegetables to play with."

Valencia opened his restaurant (named after a Mayan prophecy) in 2009, when he was just twenty-three. But his local, seasonal style of cooking is one he learned at a young age.

Though he grew up in Sonoma, California, his parents and extended family are from Mexico. He would travel there a couple of times a year as a child, often for months at a time.

"I come from a big family of farmers and ranchers," Valencia says. He would hang out in the orchard where his grandpa grows mangoes, bananas, coffee beans, limes, and other produce. He'd help his grandfather butcher goats and sheep and would watch homegrown *masa* be mashed with a large stone rolling pin to grind flour for tortillas.

"There was a lot of work that went into it," he says.

By the time he was eight, he knew he would be a chef. Later, he enrolled in the California Culinary Academy in San Francisco and landed a three-month internship under Rick Bayless at Frontera. Two months into his stay, he was hired full-time. He eventually became the sous chef at Frontera and at Bayless' Topolobampo.

"Rick has been my biggest influence, culinary-wise," he says. "I just really respect him a lot for opening it up for other chefs like me."

Valencia, like all Chicago chefs committed to local foods, has struggled with getting good produce in the winter. He cans his own tomatoes for use in sauces during the colder months. And he has sought out farmers who use greenhouses and other methods of cultivating cold-weather produce.

The women of Three Sisters have struggled with the same problem.

"The first year we had the farm, one of the first orders of business was to figure out how we were going to have income in the winter," Vowell says. They built a greenhouse, which allows for year-round production. And they constructed hoop houses for their tomatoes.

"The tenacity of Mother Nature was a really big discovery for me," she says. Rather than fighting with insects and diseases, "we kind of choose our crops according to the pest thing," she says.

In one of the early years, Vowel remembers planting some 1,500 tomato seedlings two days before the last frost date. And, of course, the weather turned frigid and all of the seedlings died.

"I was out at 2 or 3 a.m., using the headlights on the car, trying to cover things up," Vowell says. "Let me just go up to the roof and jump off."

Yes, farming is hard work. But Vowell says she wouldn't trade this life for the hectic one back in the kitchen.

She recalled a day when the Frontera staff was brought outside on a sunny afternoon for a group photo. The cooks all had to shield their eyes from the light because they'd become so accustomed to working indoors.

"I was not living a sustainable lifestyle," she says. "Life was too hard, too mentally draining. There were too many things happening every day I was unaware of.

"I have a massive maple tree in the yard. It loses its leaves in twenty-four to thirty-six hours. It doesn't piddle around. I like being aware of the fact that the tree loses its leaves so fast."

Tracey's Black Bean Soup
with Squash Blossom Quesadilla
From Chuy Valencia of Chilam Balam

SOUP

- 2 c. Three Sisters black beans
- 8 c. water
- 1 tsp. unrefined pork lard
- 1 medium sweet onion, thinly sliced
- 4 cloves sweet garlic, roasted
- 1/2 Three Sisters habanero
- 8 leaves of Three Sisters epazote

Simmer the beans in water and lard until tender and the liquid is rich and slightly thick. In a sauté pan over medium-low heat, caramelize the onion and garlic until very sweet. Blend with some of the black bean stock but not any of the beans. Strain into a pot and add the habanero and epazote wrapped in cheesecloth so it can be easily pulled out later. Blend the rest of the beans and stock but only slightly to leave sort of chunky. Add to the pot and continue to simmer until a chowderlike consistency is achieved. Pull out the habanero and epazote and season with salt to taste.

QUESADILLA

- 8 Three Sisters squash blossoms
- 2 large corn tortillas approximately 10 in., homemade if possible
- 4 oz. shredded jack cheese, preferably Nordic Creamery
- 1 oz. chopped Three Sisters epazote

Remove the pistils from the blossoms and tear the yellow flowers into big pieces. Heat a large flat sauté pan or griddle on medium and lay the tortilla down, sprinkle 2 oz. of cheese evenly on one half, along with half of the epazote and blossoms. Once the tortilla is pliable, about a minute, fold over and flip it. Toast about 3 minutes per side until cheese is melted. Serve with soup.

Oatmeal Pecan Cookies

From Tracey Vowell of Three Sisters

  1/2 lb. butter, softened
  1 c. firmly packed brown sugar
  1/2 c. sugar
  2 eggs
  1 tsp. vanilla
  3 c. rolled oats
  1 dash cayenne, or other moderately hot dried pepper
  1 1/2 c. flour
  1 tsp. baking soda
  1/2 tsp. salt
  1/2 c. roasted pecans, chopped
  1/2 c. dried cherries, blueberries, or raisins

Preheat oven to 350°F. Lightly grease two cookie sheets with oil or butter.

Using a mixer, cream the butter and sugars together until light and fluffy. Add the eggs and vanilla, mix until incorporated.

Using a spice grinder or food processor, pulverize one cup of the oats to a fine meal, stir the oats together with the cayenne, flour, baking soda, and salt. Slowly add the dry ingredients to the mixer bowl with the mixer on low. Mix until thoroughly incorporated, 1–2 minutes. Add the remaining oats, pecans, and cherries and mix just enough to form a thoroughly moist mass. Using a tablespoon, drop slightly heaping spoonfuls onto the cookie sheets, allowing a bit of space between for the cookies to flatten as they bake. Bake 10–12 minutes, or until cookies begin to brown around the edges. Allow the cookies to cool on the sheet a bit before transferring to a rack.

Butternut Polenta

with Bacon and Mushrooms

From Tracey Vowell of Three Sisters

  1 small butternut squash
  4 c. milk
  1 tbsp. salt
  1 c. cornmeal (either coarse or fine)
  1–2 c. water
  1/2 lb. thick-sliced bacon
  1/2 lb. shiitake or oyster mushrooms
  2–3 oz. mixed microgreens

Remove the stem from the squash and split in half from top to bottom. Remove the seeds and place the squash, cut side down, onto a sheet pan. Place in a 350°F oven and bake about 45 minutes, or until well softened. Reduce the oven to 300°F.

Allow the squash to cool a bit, then peel off the skin and measure out 3 c. of flesh into a bowl and mash a bit with a potato masher. It does not need to be completely smooth. Set aside.

Heat the milk and salt in a fairly large saucepan over medium-high heat until steamy and beginning to boil. Stir once or twice as the milk heats to prevent scorching. Slowly add the cornmeal to the milk, stirring constantly with a whisk to avoid lumps. Reduce the heat to medium and continue stirring as the mixture thickens. Add the squash and stir in well.

Pour about 1/2–3/4 c. water over the corn mixture and stir in, then cover the pan and place in the oven. Check every 12–15 minutes, stirring thoroughly and adding small quantities of water as needed, cooking a total of 40–45 minutes.

Slice the bacon into sticks, more or less, and cook in a skillet until well-browned and crisp. While the bacon cooks, stem and roughly slice the mushrooms. Remove the bacon to a paper-towel–lined dish when done, and pour off all but a couple of tablespoons of the rendered fat. Add the mushrooms to the already heated pan and cook on high until thoroughly cooked. Season with salt.

Spoon the polenta into a serving dish, sprinkle on the bacon and mushrooms, consider grating a bit of dry cheese over everything, and finish off with a good handful of microgreens.

Wisconsin Trout "Tamal"

with Huitlacoche and Fresh Goat Cheese

From Chuy Valencia of Chilam Balam

TROUT AND FILLING

1 ear Three Sisters sweet corn, husked
1/2 large red onion, sliced into 1/4-inch-thick rounds
4 cloves sweet garlic
4 oz. Three Sisters huitlacoche kernels
6 leaves of Three Sisters epazote
1/2 c. soft goat cheese
1/2 c. cow's milk ricotta
2 12-oz. Rushing Waters (or other farm-fresh) trout fillets
4 fresh Three Sisters corn husks

Grill the corn, red onion, and garlic cloves on medium heat until the corn and onion are lightly charred and softened. The garlic should be just toasted in color and spongy. Set aside. In a wide sauté pan, heat a tiny bit of vegetable oil on high heat and toss in the huitlacoche. Little by little, add handfuls of water so it begins to steam and become inky. Once very dark and somewhat dry, transfer to a mixing bowl and cool.

Remove the kernels from the corn; finely chop the onion, garlic, and epazote and add it to the huitlacoche. Mix in the soft goat cheese and ricotta until creamy and well distributed. Add salt to taste.

Clean any pin bones from the trout fillets, lay flat, flesh side up, and season lightly with salt. Lay some spoonfuls of the mixture down on one side of the fillet, about 4–5 oz., and fold the other fillet over to close it. Overlap two corn husks with the wider part on the inside to achieve a sort of hammock shape for the fish. Lay fish in the center and wrap just enough to secure the fish but not overly tightening it. With some strips of the same husk, tie the small ends and the middle of the package to secure the husk. Heat a shallow pan on a hot burner and toast on one side 3–4 minutes until the leaf chars slightly. Flip, then place in 500°F oven for 8 minutes.

SALSA

8 large tomatillos, husked and rinsed
1/2 large Three Sisters red onion
2 cloves sweet garlic
2 serrano chilies, or to taste
1/4 bunch cilantro
1 lime, juice only
Salt, to taste

Roast everything, except cilantro and lime, over medium heat in a grill pan. The tomatillos should be charred and juicy, the rest of the ingredients equally charred and softened. Dice the tomatillos roughly, reserving the juice and all; finely mince the onion, garlic, and chilies, and chiffonade the cilantro. Place all ingredients in a mixing bowl and season with salt and lime juice. The mixture should be spicy, salty, and refreshing.

To serve, slit the husk lengthwise and open to expose the skin side of the fish, lightly brûlée the skin under the broiler or with a kitchen torch to crisp it. Spoon some of the salsa diagonally over it and garnish with chunks of grilled corn and goat cheese.

Floriole Café & Bakery

Chef Sandra Holl

Ellis Family Farms

At least four generations of René Gelder's family have been farmers, and that's just in America. She can trace her family's farming lineage even farther in Europe.

Gelder, of Ellis Family Farms, now lives in Benton Harbor, Michigan, in the farmhouse once owned by her maternal grandparents. Shortly after Gelder and her husband, Bruce, were married, her grandmother moved to a nursing home. The farm was in jeopardy: Her parents planned to tear it down unless the Gelders wanted to take it on.

"I could never get rid of the farm," she says. But the house needed significant upgrades.

"We started doing a little remodeling," Gelder says. And then they realized there "were just bare wires behind the walls. They traded fruit and got their flooring or they traded fruit and got their wiring."

Decades later, that's sort of how Gelder met Sandra Holl of Floriole Bakery. The two saw each other at a farmers' market at the Museum of Contemporary Art about five years ago, when Gelder traded Holl some fruit for some of her rustic baked goods.

"She was just starting out," Gelder recalls.

Gelder's grandparents, who moved to the United States from the Ukraine, began growing fruit during the Great Depression. When her father took over the farm in the late 1960s, he started growing some 60 acres of tomatoes. And when Gelder and her husband became more involved with the farm in the 1980s, they began growing green beans on 50 acres. They no longer grow beans, focusing instead on fruit (peaches and apples are their prime crops) and honey.

Gelder, a former teacher, has zeroed in on researching ways to make her farm more sustainable and environmentally friendly.

"In the past ten years, we've gone more sustainable than my dad ever thought we could," she says. "In the 1970s, you sprayed every seven days, no matter what. We've probably decreased 75 percent of the pesticides."

Gelder and her family currently have 58 acres, a good chunk of it preserved in natural grass and flowers to colonize the bumblebees. Gelder purchases tens of thousands of bumblebees, who help shake the pollen from the blueberry bushes. "We've found almost quadruple the yield for blueberries using bumblebees versus honeybees," she says. (Honeybees have a hard time getting the nectar out of the blueberry.)

Just as Gelder has grown her farm, Holl has grown her bakery business. Holl, who once worked in marketing and as an English teacher in France, decided to go back to school to study pastry.

After school, she worked at Tartine Bakery in San Francisco.

"That's where I learned a whole lot about sourcing locally and using fresh ingredients," Holl says.

Holl, whose husband is French, came to Chicago to visit family while waiting for her husband to get his green card.

"The green card took a long time," she says. "I fell in love with the city and with the Green City Market, especially."

She started making pastries like her homey, flaky galettes, out of Kitchen Chicago, a shared rental commercial kitchen space. And she began selling them at the market to rave reviews.

"What we do is pretty darn simple," she says. "We're trying not to do too much to the flavors of the fruit or the vegetables. Everything is pretty rustic. If your grandma baked, I would imagine she would make this stuff."

And in March 2010, Floriole opened a bright, airy two-story bakery/dining space with seventy-three seats and an open-for-viewing kitchen.

"We're going to be cranking out a lot of pastry," Holl says. "But it still has kind of a quaint feeling."

Caramels

From Sandra Holl of Floriole Café & Bakery

2 c. sugar
1/2 tsp. salt
1 tbsp. honey
Water, enough to make mixture sandy
1 pt. cream
2 oz. butter
Sea salt, to garnish

In a heavy-bottomed pot, cook sugar, salt, honey, and water until it is medium-dark amber. Remove from heat and add cream. (Mixture will sputter and bubble.) Whisk in butter until emulsified. Using a candy thermometer, return to 248°F–250°F. Pour into small loaf pans that have been buttered and lined with parchment paper. Sprinkle with sea salt. Cut as desired.

Honey Raspberry Sauce

From René Gelder of Ellis Family Farms

2 c. fresh raspberries (strained to remove seeds, if desired)
1/4 c. honey
2 tbsp. brandy, if making dessert sauce

Puree berries and stir in honey and brandy, if desired. Spoon sauce on top of chicken or pork during roasting. Or, use as a topping for ice cream or angel food cake. The sauce can also be used as filling for a layer cake.

Simple Honey Tea (Iced)

From René Gelder of Ellis Family Farms

2 bags tea (green or black)
1/2 c. fresh mint leaves
1/4 c. honey
4 c. boiling water

In a heatproof pitcher, place tea, mint, and honey along with the boiling water. Let steep for 5 minutes. Remove mint leaves and tea bags. Let cool. Serve over ice.

Almond Pound Cake
with Lemon-Lavender Glaze

From Sandra Holl of Floriole Café & Bakery

Makes 1 cake

- 6 tbsp. almond paste
- 3 1/2 oz. butter
- 3/4 c. plus 1 tbsp. sugar
- 3 eggs
- Juice and zest from 1 lemon
- 1/2 tsp. salt
- 1 c. flour
- 3/4 tsp. baking powder
- 1/2 c. sliced almonds

Preheat oven to 350°F. Break up almond paste. Cream together almond paste with butter and sugar. Add eggs one by one. Add lemon juice, zest, and salt. Fold in flour and baking powder. Fill a 9x5-in. loaf pan three-quarters full and top with sliced almonds. Bake in preheated oven for 40 minutes or until done.

Lemon-Lavender Glaze

- 1/3 c. lemon juice
- 1/4 c. honey
- 1 tbsp. lavender

Combine all ingredients in a small saucepan and bring to a simmer. Remove cake from pan and let cool for about half an hour. Brush the glaze onto the cake, making sure to include the sides and bottom.

Naha

Chef Carrie Nahabedian
Green Acres Farm

One is a celebrated chef and the other is a farmer, but Carrie Nahabedian and Beth Eccles have one important thing in common: They both come from immigrant families that taught them a deep love and respect for food.

Eccles, who runs North Judson, Indiana-based Green Acres Farm with her husband, Brent, sells a wide variety of produce to Nahabedian's upscale downtown restaurant, Naha. Both women serve on the board of the Green City Market.

Nahabedian's grandparents fled Turkey during the Armenian genocide of the early 1900s and found safety in America.

"We didn't eat prepared foods, we didn't eat packaged foods," Nahabedian says during a post-lunch-rush break at Naha. "Everyone in the family was highly accomplished. Everyone was a great cook."

Nahabedian grew up in Chicago and knew at a young age that food would be her life. As a teenager, she worked as a prep cook at Chicago's Ritz-Carlton Hotel. She later worked at some of the city's finest restaurants before moving to California in 1991 to become executive chef of the Four Seasons in Santa Barbara.

Working in California opened her eyes to local food. "Everything came from a farmer," Nahabedian says. "You take a carrot down there and juice it and you get a whole glass of juice. It was just eye-opening.

"You knew all the seasons. You could actually say how long of a stem you wanted on your artichokes."

Nahabedian was pleased when she returned to Chicago in 2000 to see a flourishing local-foods movement. She credited this largely to Abby Mandel, who founded Chicago's Green City Market in 1998 with just nine farmers that year. Mandel died in 2008, leaving behind a hugely popular farmers' market that draws more than 100,000 visitors a year.

"It wasn't a trend," Nahabedian says. "It wasn't a cycle. It was just people doing the right thing. The city has truly embraced it. We're lucky to be in a region that supports its own."

Each year brings new treats from farmers that she can serve at Naha, she says. It's a winning collaboration for both chefs and farmers.

"[Farmers] enjoy the status they're at, and they enjoy the fact that the chefs are proud to have their products in their restaurants," she says.

Eccles, whose maiden name is Sakaguchi, grew up on the farm, which was started by her Japanese-immigrant grandparents. Her grandparents were sharecroppers and operated a small whole-sale business, selling Asian produce to stores in Chinatown and small restaurants on Argyle Street. They grew Japanese radishes and Chinese bitter melon and sold them off the back of their truck. Eccles' father continued the farm, selling exclusively Asian vegetables to restaurants around Chicago.

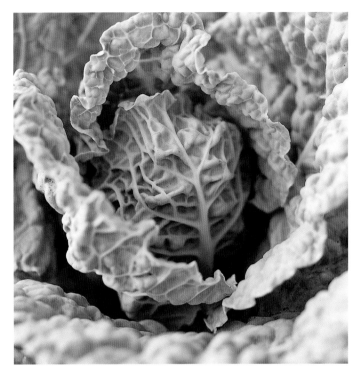

Eccles hadn't planned on getting into the family business. She was working for a group of philosophers at Purdue University, and her husband had no farming background. But in 1996 a farm went up for sale 3 miles from her grandparents' old farm. They decided it would be a great way to be near family, doing something they loved.

She started selling some of the Asian vegetables at farmers' markets and was wowed by the response.

"We just couldn't believe how excited people were about the vegetables," she says. "It was so rewarding to have people who were interested in what we were doing."

The Eccles now own 155 acres. They grow about 600 varieties of produce on about 30 acres each year.

"As I look back, I think we must've been crazy," she says. "We didn't really have a plan. It was very challenging in the beginning."

The Eccles sell produce to some seventy chefs each week. They've expanded way beyond Asian vegetables. Their biggest sellers now are their eighty varieties of heirloom tomatoes, a dozen different cucumbers, eight types of summer squash, and six kinds of eggplant, among others.

The Eccles have two daughters, one a teenager and the other still in elementary school. The younger daughter likes to tool around the farm in a golf cart, picking out kale and other vegetables to munch on. The older daughter helps out at markets.

"She's one of my top sellers," Eccles says. "She's great with people and her math is excellent. And she likes it. She likes living on a farm."

Yukon Potato Gnocchi, Tomatoes, Roasted Eggplant, and Spinach

Yukon Potato Gnocchi, Tomatoes, Roasted Eggplant, and Spinach

with a "Fondue" of Ricotta Cheese and Fresh-squeezed Tomato Broth

From Chef Carrie Nahabedian of Naha

Serves 8

12 Yukon gold potatoes

2 eggs

Kosher salt and black pepper, to taste

4 c. all-purpose flour

3/4 c. olive oil, divided

1 eggplant, cut into 2-in. chunks

3 thyme sprigs

2 lb. good-quality fresh tomatoes, pureed with a splash of water and sieved to remove pulp and seeds (enough to make 2 c. of juice)

1 lb. fava beans, peeled and blanched, membrane removed

2 ripe heirloom tomatoes, cut into small wedges

1/2 c. basil leaves, torn

4 oz. pea shoots

1 bunch spinach

1 c. good-quality ricotta cheese

2 tbsp. butter

Cook the potatoes in water until just tender. Remove from water and quickly remove the skins. Place on a pan and dry the potatoes out for 2 minutes in a preheated 350°F oven. Cool slightly. Run the potatoes through a ricer or grate them coarsely.

Place potatoes on the work area or cutting board. Add eggs. Season with kosher salt and cracked black pepper. Set aside 4 c. of flour. Place 3 c. of the flour on the work area and make a well. Add in the potato mixture and work dough with your hands. It takes time, but do not overwork the dough. Add flour as needed; dough should be slightly dry, not wet. Let rest for 15 minutes, covered with a towel.

Cut a piece off the dough. Roll it by hand into a large rope. Cut the gnocchi into 1/2-in. pieces. You can also choose to roll with a fork for more detail. Make sure the cutting board/work area is dusted with flour. Place raw gnocchi on a parchment-lined pan and keep rolling out the rest. You can freeze gnocchi at this point in an airtight plastic container that is lined with parchment that has been dusted with cornmeal or flour.

Cook gnocchi in boiling salted water with 1/8 c. of olive oil until the gnocchi "float." Remove with a slotted spoon and cool on a pan. Lightly toss with 1/8 c. of olive oil. Let cool.

Toss the cut eggplant with 1/4 c. olive oil, kosher salt, black pepper, and a few thyme sprigs. Place on a roasting pan and roast in a 450°F oven until a rich golden brown with crispy skin. Set aside.

Marinate the heirloom tomato wedges in 1/4 c. olive oil, along with the torn basil leaves, kosher salt, and pepper. Chill.

Clean and reserve pea shoots for the garnish. Clean and reserve 1 bunch of spinach.

In a nonstick sauté pan, lightly brown the gnocchi in butter which has started to brown. Cook gnocchi until lightly colored on all sides. Add in all the ingredients except the marinated tomatoes, tomato juice, and ricotta cheese. Wilt the spinach and season to taste. Melt in the ricotta and add the tomato juice and marinated tomatoes.

"Griddled" Julianna Goat Cheese Sandwich with a Salad of Big Leaf Spinach, Shaved Nectarines and Fennel, Celery Root Scented with Apple Mint, and Yogurt Grain Mustard

From Carrie Nahabedian of Naha

Serves 8

2 c. fresh-pressed apple cider

2 tbsp. grain mustard

1/4–1/2 c. extra-virgin olive oil, to make an emulsified vinaigrette (depends on amount of cider syrup used)

1 tbsp. apple cider vinegar

1 piece of celery root, peeled and julienned

1/2 pt. good-quality plain yogurt or goat's milk yogurt

2 tbsp. blossom honey

1 tbsp. apple mint, chiffonaded (can use mint)

1 piece Capriole Farm Julianna cheese (or other good-quality goat cheese)

1/4 loaf brioche, sliced thin

2 tbsp. butter

4 nectarines, slightly firm, thinly shaved

1 bulb of fennel, shaved

2 lbs. Big Leaf or baby spinach, cleaned and dried Kosher salt and cracked black pepper, to taste.

Reduce the apple cider over medium-high heat until it is a rich and viscous syrup. Set aside.

In a stainless-steel bowl using a whisk, make vinaigrette using the mustard, half of the cider syrup, oil, and vinegar. Reserve the other half of the cider syrup for a drizzle on the salad before serving.

Mix the celery root with the yogurt, honey, and apple mint to make a rémoulade. Set aside.

Slice the Julianna cheese and make into sandwiches with the brioche. "Griddle" them in a sauté pan over low heat with butter, as for grilled-cheese sandwiches. Brown nicely on both sides and pat dry. Trim crusts and cut into wedges. Keep warm if possible.

Using a mandoline, shave the nectarines and fennel into a bowl. Add the spinach. Toss with the vinaigrette. Place on plates and top the salad with the celery root rémoulade. Drizzle with the reserved apple cider syrup and serve with the sandwiches.

Coddled Egg, Prosciutto, and Ramps with White Corn Polenta, Goat Cheese, Watercress, and Radishes

From Carrie Nahabedian of Naha

Serves 8

- 1 1/2 c. white cornmeal
- 4 c. water
- 4 oz. soft butter, divided
- Salt and cracked black pepper, to taste
- 1/2 c. heavy cream
- 16 pieces ramps (wild leeks)
- 4 tbsp. extra-virgin olive oil, divided
- 1/2 lb. La Quercia prosciutto, sliced thin
- 1/2 piece Sofia goat cheese (whole loaf) or similar cheese (1 oz. per person), divided
- 8 whole farm eggs
- 1/2 lb. radishes, shaved
- 1 lb. watercress
- 2 tbsp. parsley, chopped
- 1 tbsp. red wine vinegar

Preheat the oven to 350°F.

Mix the cornmeal with 2 c. of cold water. Bring the other 2 c. of water to a boil, add half of the butter, and season with salt and pepper. Add in the white cornmeal. Stir, stir, and stir. Use a heavy wooden spoon, preferably with a flat end, and stir constantly over medium heat for about 20 minutes. Add the cream. Add half of the goat cheese. If necessary, you can make the polenta richer and add more butter. Taste again and adjust seasoning. Keep warm with a buttered piece of waxed paper on top.

Clean the ramps by trimming the base of the ramp, root end, and washing thoroughly. Pat dry. Drizzle with extra-virgin olive oil and roast quickly, approximately 5 minutes in the oven. Reserve and keep warm.

For the eggs, butter the ramekins you will be cooking the eggs in. Line the buttered egg ramekins with a slice of prosciutto and a small piece of Sofia goat cheese, and then crack the egg on top. Season lightly with salt and cracked black pepper. Bake in a water bath until the egg is soft-cooked, or coddled, approximately 6 minutes.

While the eggs are cooking, make a salad of the shaved radishes, watercress and parsley. Drizzle with the red wine vinegar. Place a spoon of polenta on each serving plate, place ramps on top. Carefully spoon the egg from the ramekin atop the ramps. Serve with the salad.

Signature Room at the 95th

Chef Patrick Sheerin

Shooting Star Farm

If location is everything, it's hard to top Chef Patrick Sheerin. Cooking out of his "kitchen in the clouds," Sheerin is the chef at the Signature Room at the 95th, the fine-dining restaurant near the top of the John Hancock Center. He'll serve 3,000 diners during a typical weekend. And yet he remains committed to sourcing local, seasonal ingredients.

"Number one, it just tastes better," Sheerin says. "I really believe in the relationship we have with our planet. With our buying power, if I buy all of the unique stuff, they'll grow more. And it just increases the biodiversity. It's the right thing to do."

Sheerin grew up in Chicago. He remembers visiting his grand-parents' sprawling garden in the suburbs.

"Only one strip of area in front of my grandparents' house was safe for flowers," he says. "Every other area was used." Pear and apple trees lined the garage. There were tomatoes, spaghetti squash, green beans, and beets. "Just an amazing amount of stuff," he says.

For several seasons, Sheerin carpooled to the farmers' market with Chef Paul Virant of Vie, cramming their vehicle with as much local produce as it would hold. "He and I would have long conversations about [local food]," Sheerin says.

When the car got too full, Sheerin started taking a cab. "One day I needed two cabs to get everything back to the restaurant," he says. "We're a big restaurant. Every Wednesday and Saturday I was having to do this."

Now the farmers come to Sheerin, though he still loves strolling through the market. He receives deliveries of local produce six days a week.

Buying locally grown food in such large quantities has helped Sheerin keep kitchen costs in check. Plus, there's less waste because the produce is so fresh, he says, "The shelf life is too unreal."

He encourages chefs who are just beginning to source locally grown foods to pick one or two ingredients for each season. Focus on those and find your favorites, he recommends.

"For us, we started with asparagus," he says. "The difference is profound. The asparagus is sweet. The nuance of it is just unreal."

Every time a new ingredient comes into the kitchen, Sheerin talks about it with his cooks. And several times a month, he discusses the local foods with his front-of-the-house staff.

"They like to tell the story," he says. "That's an important part of using local food. Some people don't think it's very sexy, but with locally grown stuff, there's always a story."

And one of those stories is Rink DaVee, a cook-turned-farmer. DaVee and Sheerin went to the same high school, Chicago's St. Ignatius, though at different times.

More than twenty years ago, DaVee worked for Alice Waters at the famed Chez Panisse restaurant in Berkeley, California. The experience transformed him.

"It opened my eyes to farming," he says. "I have, for the last twenty years, been on the other side of the process of getting great food to people. It did stem from working in a restaurant and seeing a moment that happens with great chefs like Patrick or Alice Waters, who recognize that food does not start when it comes in the back door. It starts on the farm. The quality of their dishes starts on the farm."

DaVee moved from California to Wisconsin in 1991, where he apprenticed on a farm and soon bought his own land. In 1996, he and his wife bought their farm, Shooting Star Farm, near Mineral Point, Wisconsin. They now farm about 5 acres of certified-organic mixed vegetables. About 80 percent of what he produces goes to Chicago restaurants.

Sheerin regularly buys microgreens from Shooting Star Farm and especially likes their winter vegetables, such as rutabagas and turnips.

"I grow food so people will eat it," DaVee says. "It's a process that starts with me. It's not complete until somebody takes a bite of it."

DaVee and his wife have a young son who already loves picking up a hoe and heading to the field. He hopes that passion for local food will grow in future generations.

"We have a revolution of sorts in the country where people are questioning whether not knowing where their food comes from is really sound judgment on our part," he says. "The conventional food system is very opaque. It's very opaque, and we're part of a movement that's about transparency."

Spice-braised Market Root Vegetables with Jasmine Rice and Sesame Broth

From Patrick Sheerin
of Signature Room at the 95th

Serves 4

BRAISED VEGETABLES

8 carrots, peeled with a little of the top left on
1/2 ginger knob, grated
1 tbsp. agave nectar
Salt, to taste
1 tbsp. butter

1 rutabaga, peeled and cut into 1-in. planks that will be cut
  into diamonds after they cook
1 orange, zested
1/4 tsp. toasted ground fennel seeds
Salt, to taste
1 tbsp. butter

1 lb. Japanese sweet potatoes, cut into 3/4-in. rounds
1/4 tsp. toasted and lightly ground cumin seeds
Salt, to taste
1 tbsp. butter

3/4 lb. celery root, sliced
Salt, to taste
1 tbsp. butter

Preheat oven to 375°F. Prepare each vegetable for roasting, in separate pans, with the listed ingredients. Roast each combination in a small pan covered with foil until tender. Different vegetables will have different cooking times.

4 cippolini onions, peeled
1 star anise pod
Water
Salt, to taste
1 tbsp. butter

Place peeled onions in a small sauté pan. Add star anise and enough water to halfway cover onions. Cook down to a glaze. Add salt and butter.

8–12 baby turnips, blanched in boiling salted water

JASMINE RICE AND SESAME BROTH

1/2 white onion, thinly sliced

1/4 c. canola oil

1/2 c. Madeira wine

1/4 c. sesame seeds, toasted until golden brown

1/4 c. jasmine rice, toasted in a 350°F oven until golden brown

4 c. vegetable stock

2 jasmine tea balls (available online or at specialty stores) or jasmine tea bags

1 tbsp. toasted sesame seed oil

Sauté the onions in canola oil until soft, deglaze with Madeira, and cook until evaporated. Add the sesame seeds, rice, and vegetable stock, and simmer. When the rice is soft, add the jasmine tea in a sachet and let steep for 4 minutes (but no longer or it will become bitter). Pull out the tea, stir, and adjust seasoning. The rice and broth should have the consistency of cold cream; add more vegetable stock to thin, if necessary. Drizzle with toasted sesame seed oil.

SEASONED YOGURT SAUCE

1 c. whole-milk Greek yogurt

1/4 c. buttermilk

4 kaffir lime leaves, sliced

1/2-in. knob fresh turmeric, grated

Lime juice and zest

3 tbsp. olive oil

1/16 tsp. xanthan gum

Handful of Thai basil leaves

2 radishes, thinly sliced

1 tbsp. olive oil

1 tsp. lemon juice

Salt, to taste

Combine yogurt, buttermilk, and kaffir lime leaves in a saucepan. Bring to a boil. Add the turmeric and remove from heat. Let stand 30 minutes. Remove the lime leaves and drain through several layers of cheesecloth. Refrigerate overnight.

Puree the mixture in a blender. Adjust seasoning with a touch of salt, lime zest, and lime juice. Emulsify with olive oil. Add the xanthan gum and puree. Pour the sauce through a fine-mesh sieve. To serve· Warm the vegetables in a single layer in a 200°F oven. Ladle 1 oz. toasted rice and sesame broth in the bottom of four bowls. Divide the vegetables among the bowls. Place a ribbon of yogurt on the vegetables.

Toss basil leaves and radishes with olive oil, lemon juice, and a little salt. Sprinkle mixture in the middle of each bowl.

Summer Watermelon Salad

From Patrick Sheerin of Signature Room at the 95th

Serves 8

1 whole watermelon, seedless

1 lemon, zest and juice

1 tbsp. extra-virgin olive oil

Pickled watermelon rind (recipe follows)

8 oz. sheep's milk feta cheese, crumbled

4 oz. baby arugula

1 bunch fresh-picked oregano

Salt and pepper, to taste

Cut the top and bottom off the watermelon. Cut down the sides to release the flesh. Reserve the rind. Cut the watermelon into planks and shingle on a large serving plate.

Dress with lemon zest, lemon juice, and extra-virgin olive oil. Scatter pickled watermelon rind over the top, along with feta, arugula, and oregano. Season with salt and pepper.

PICKLED WATERMELON RIND

2 lb. watermelon rind

3 c. clear, distilled vinegar

2 tbsp. kosher salt, plus more for soaking solution

1 c. water, plus more for soaking rind

5 c. sugar

1 tbsp. whole dried chilies

1 tbsp. whole coriander seeds

1 tbsp. whole cumin seeds

Remove all of the green and pink portions from the watermelon rind. Cut into small pieces and soak in water with 5 percent salt added, by weight, for at least an hour. Drain and rinse the watermelon rind.

Combine vinegar, 2 tbsp. salt, 1 c. water, sugar, and spices in a heavy saucepan or stock pot. Stir well. Heat the syrup to simmering. Remove from heat, cover, and steep for 1 hour to extract the flavor from the spices.

Boil the syrup and reduce by one-quarter. Pour syrup over watermelon rind and cool to room temperature. Place in refrigerator overnight before serving. It will keep for 2 weeks.

Sunday Dinner

Chefs Joshua Kulp and Christine Cikowski
Seedling Orchard

"I'm the dude who freaked out and bought an orchard," says Peter Klein, the owner of South Haven, Michigan-based Seedling Orchard.

Klein isn't kidding. He had a career in restaurant marketing in Chicago, but Klein's true passion lived at the farmers' market. He'd get there early and buy all that he could.

"I fell in love with the product," Klein says.

And then he heard that his "favorite fruit guys" were retiring. Thoughts of purchasing their farm immediately entered his mind. But he'd never farmed before, and the business was far from his home in Chicago.

"I thought, 'That's a really bad idea,'" Klein says. "So I decided to do a business plan and see if it makes sense. And I said, 'It's a really, really bad idea.'"

Still, that didn't stop him from buying the 80-acre plot, which had been a farm as long as anyone could recall.

"It was a beautifully maintained property," Klein says. Plus, the farm's longtime foreman stayed on to help.

"You learn pretty quick over the first couple of years," he adds.

Klein has met several of his clients through the Green City Market, including the chefs behind Sunday Dinner, Josh Kulp and Christine Cikowski.

Sunday Dinner follows an unusual model. It's a supper club of sorts, a private "community" of about 1,300 diners who can choose to attend dinners in other members' homes. Each person on the list must be invited by someone else in the club.

Each month, Kulp and Cikowski e-mail a menu ("basic, seasonal cuisine," Kulp calls it) to the list of diners. They put on six to twelve dinners per month, with about fifteen to twenty guests at each one.

"An hour later, we've sold it out," Kulp says. "The people who come to our dinners are just people who are really interested in the style of dining. Most of them are repeat diners."

The two then prepare some of the meal at Kitchen Chicago, a shared-use commercial kitchen, before finishing the courses at the chosen home.

"Our biggest influences are Mediterranean, Italian, Spanish, [and] Mexican food," Kulp says. "It's what we can get locally."

Cikowski has a background as a pastry chef, and Kulp focuses on the savory foods. They work out the menu together, and they try to keep the food accessible, with three-course dinners for about $40 and five- or six-course meals for $65 to $75.

"We do it really because we love it," Kulp says.

Sunday Dinner can also be hired for private functions. Kulp and Cikowski have developed a line of granola bars, Eat Green Foods, which are available in stores around Chicago. They're made from local, sustainable ingredients.

Kulp states they would love to see their granola-bar company take off so it would support the dinner-party business.

Kulp adds that Klein has been a big supporter of the dinner club.

"He's a regular diner at our dinner clubs," Kulp says. "We use his apple cider. We use a lot of his fruits in season. Whatever is in season, we'll turn into dessert. He's a very funny guy, very outgoing. And he loves food."

Grilled Peaches, Prosciutto, and Wild Gulf Shrimp

From Joshua Kulp of Sunday Dinner

Serves 4

 2 medium-sized, just-underripe Seedling Orchard peaches
 1 lb. large wild Gulf shrimp, peeled and deveined
 Sea salt
 Fresh-ground black pepper
 1/4 lb. thin-sliced La Quercia prosciutto
 4 tbsp. basil oil (recipe follows)
 1 oz. or 1 handful of pea shoots
 Juice of 1 lemon
 Extra-virgin olive oil, to drizzle

Light a charcoal grill.

Slice peaches into nice rounds about 1/4 in. thick. Be sure that your grill grates are hot and clean. Lay peach rounds on grate and grill until grill marks appear, about 20–30 seconds, and then flip. If the peaches seem to be cooking too fast, move them to a cooler spot on the grill or grill for less time.

Season shrimp with salt and pepper. Clean the grill grate, lay the shrimp on the grill in a single layer, and cook until they have nice grill marks and are an even pink color. Be careful not to overcook the shrimp.

To serve, lay one-fourth of the peaches on each plate in an even layer, and then place one-fourth of the shrimp on each plate. Add prosciutto slices and drizzle the entire dish with 1 tbsp. of basil oil. Place a small handful of pea shoots on each dish and drizzle with lemon juice, salt, pepper, and the best olive oil you can find.

Basil Oil

From Joshua Kulp of Sunday Dinner

 1 oz. or 2 handfuls basil leaves
 1/2 oz. or 1 handful Italian parsley leaves
 1 c. extra-virgin olive oil

Place herbs and 1/4 c. oil in blender. Be careful not to run the blender too long, as the leaves can warm up and turn brown. Blend herbs and oil by pulsing for 10 seconds. Pour in the rest of the oil while the blender is running. Place in a container and refrigerate.

Brussels Sprouts
with Bacon and Apple Cider
From Joshua Kulp of Sunday Dinner

Serves 4 as a side dish

1 lb. brussels sprouts
1/2 lb. bacon, cut into thick lardons
1 tbsp. butter
1 tbsp. extra-virgin olive oil
Salt and pepper, to taste
1/2 c. apple cider

To clean brussels sprouts, peel the first couple of outer leaves and slice sprouts in half lengthwise. Then slice off the bottom of the stem, leaving some of it intact to keep the sprouts from falling apart.

In a large, heavy-bottomed sauté pan, add bacon and cook over medium-low heat until bacon has fully rendered and given up its fat. Bacon should be slightly crisp. Remove bacon to a paper towel to drain, but leave the bacon fat in the pan.

Add butter and oil to the bacon fat and raise heat to medium. Add sprouts flat-side down in an even layer to pan and sear without moving sprouts until they are nicely browned, about 3 minutes. Flip sprouts and sear on second side for about 2 minutes and season lightly with salt and pepper. Add apple cider to pan and use a wooden spoon to scrape up and caramelized bits in the pan. Let cider reduce until slightly syrupy and then return bacon to pan and toss everything together. Taste for salt and pepper and serve warm.

Late-Summer Slaw
with Mutsu Apple, Radicchio, and Pecans

From Joshua Kulp of Sunday Dinner

Serves 4 as a side dish

3 large Mutsu or Granny Smith apples, sliced into julienne
  or matchsticks
1 c. radicchio, shredded
1/2 c. green cabbage, thinly shredded
1 handful of parsley leaves, roughly chopped
1/2 c. fresh pecans
2 tbsp. Apple Cider Vinaigrette (recipe follows)
Salt and pepper, to taste

Combine all ingredients in a mixing bowl and toss with vinaigrette. Season to taste with salt and pepper; serve at room temperature.

APPLE CIDER VINAIGRETTE
1 shallot, minced
1 tbsp. apple cider vinegar
1 tsp. Dijon mustard
3 tbsp. extra-virgin olive oil

Combine shallot and vinegar in a nonreactive bowl and let macerate for at least 15 minutes, up to a couple of hours. Add mustard and drizzle in olive oil while whisking until dressing thickens.

Chilled Cherry Soup

From Peter Klein of Seedling Orchard

Serves 8 as a first course

2 qt. tart cherries, pitted, with juice
1/4 c. sugar (adjust amount of sugar to taste, depending on
  sweetness of cherries)
1/2 tsp. salt
1 cinnamon stick
1 8-oz. container of sour cream
Slice of lemon

Bring the first four ingredients to a boil. Simmer for 5 minutes until cherries are soft. Blend 1/4 c. of the hot liquid with the sour cream until uniform. Incorporate the cream mixture into the soup. Chill. Garnish with lemon slice.

Handheld Strawberry Shortcake

From Peter Klein of Seedling Orchard

Serves 4

8 large strawberries
1/2 c. cream, whipped and sweetened with 1 tsp.
  powdered sugar
1/2 c. graham crackers, crushed

Trim the short end of the berry so it stands up. Scoop out much of the flesh, leaving a thin wall. Pipe or scoop whipped cream into the hollow berry. Dust with graham cracker crumbs.

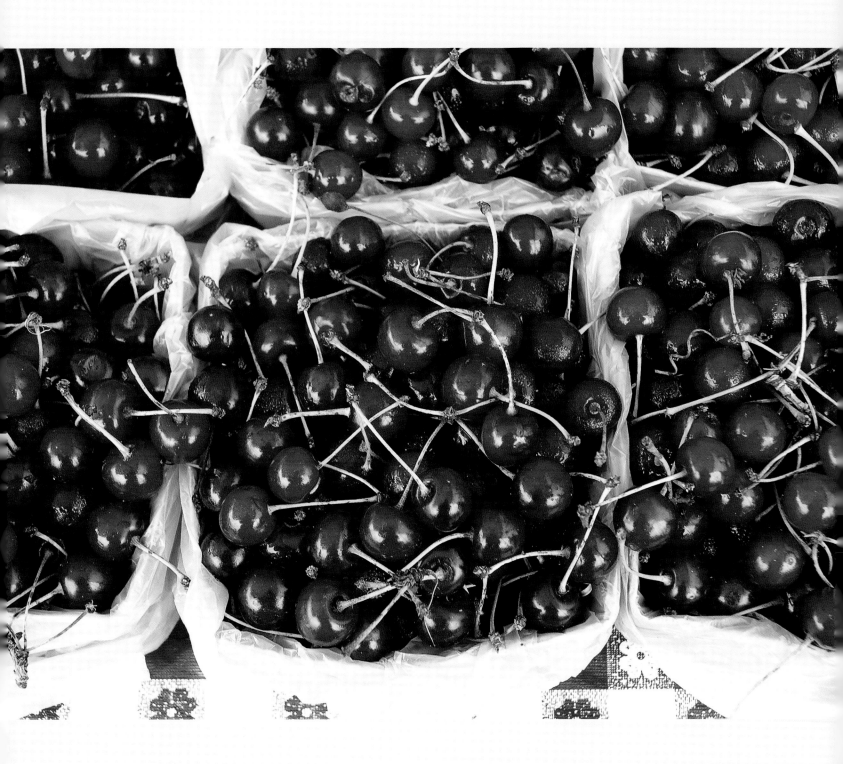

Uncommon Ground

Chef Brian Millman
Uncommon Ground Rooftop Garden

What's happening on the roof of Uncommon Ground represents the future of local food in Chicago.

The restaurant has taken its commitment to local food to the rooftop, turning potentially wasted space into 640 square feet of open soil, combined with planter boxes for growing peppers, tomatoes, beans, and other items to use in the kitchen.

"These days, there's all this talk about locavores and food miles—how far food travels to get to Chicago," says Dave Snyder, Uncommon Ground's rooftop farm director. "Around here, we like to talk about 'food steps.' From one side of the garden, it's fifty steps to the kitchen."

But there's no way Snyder could grow enough produce on the roof to sustain the restaurant. Limited square footage makes it impossible. Uncommon Ground continues to work closely with a number of local farmers. Planting on the roof was simply a way of finding a good use for some land that typically goes unused.

"If you have space, then you should use it and use it productively," Snyder says.

Snyder had been helping run Ginkgo Organic Gardens, a community food pantry garden in Chicago, for about seven years. That garden produces between a half to three-quarters of a ton of produce for donation each season, Snyder says.

"That's where I learned about growing and about gardening," he says.

Now, Snyder works on top of Uncommon Ground, planting seedlings, cultivating the plants, and educating the restaurant's customers about the project.

"I'm more of a farmer than a gardener," he says. "I have a client—the chef—and I have to make sure everything I'm growing is suitable for him. We're going to emphasize bell peppers, heirloom tomatoes, pole beans and bush beans, cooking greens. We're going to see how this project evolves.

"The vision of this rooftop garden isn't just growing peppers. We just want to prove that it's possible and see what we can figure out."

The restaurant hosts a small weekly farmers' market in the summer and offers tours of the rooftop garden during that time.

Brian Millman is the executive chef behind all of this local-food love. He has worked in restaurants most of his life and came to Uncommon Ground in 2006. He is now chef at the restaurant's two locations, both on the North Side of the city.

Local foods, he says, "are something I've always believed in but never had the full opportunity to pursue" until landing in his current job.

He looks for organic products and changes his menu several times a week.

"It helps us stay extremely seasonal," he says. "What we're putting in our bodies and what we're eating scares me sometimes. What we're serving is very wholesome, healthy ingredients. Yes, it's more expensive, but at the same time, it's kind of a moral issue of what are you serving to people. If my name is on it, it better taste good, and it better be something I would eat and I would let my wife eat."

As a chef, he loves the unparalleled freshness he can get with his mini-farm on the roof.

"We can pick [the vegetables] and use them right away," he says. "Sometimes, we find something that's so good, we don't want to do anything to it. We try to figure out ways to manipulate it a little bit to make it really, really good. We don't want to work too hard messing things up."

Crispy Chicken Breast

Crispy Chicken Breast

with Summer Bacon Succotash, Corn Puree, and Heirloom Tomatoes

From Brian Millman of Uncommon Ground

Serves 4

CORN PUREE

- 1/4 yellow onion, diced
- 1/4 small carrot, diced
- 1/4 celery rib, diced
- 1/4 jalapeño, sliced
- 1/2 tsp. minced garlic
- 1/2 c. white wine
- 2 c. corn
- Whole milk to cover
- Salt and white pepper, to taste

Sweat onions, carrots, celery, jalapeño, and garlic together. Deglaze with white wine and cook until evaporated. Add corn and milk and bring to a boil. Puree in blender and strain through a fine strainer. Season with salt and white pepper to taste.

CRISPY CHICKEN BREAST

- 4 skin-on chicken breasts
- Salt and pepper, as needed

Preheat oven to 400°F. Season chicken breast with salt and pepper and place in hot sauté pan with the skin side down. Cook until skin is golden brown and beginning to crisp. Flip chicken over and place pan in oven. Bake until chicken breast registers 165°F. Let the chicken sit for a few minutes before serving.

SUMMER BACON SUCCOTASH

- 1/4 c. thick-sliced slab bacon
- 1 tsp. minced garlic
- 1/4 c. onions, diced
- 1/4 c. red peppers, diced
- 1/2 c. corn
- 1.4 c. green beans (blanched)

Cook slab bacon in sauté pan until crispy and then remove from pan, leaving the rendered fat in the pan. Add the garlic, onions, and peppers, and sauté for about 1 minute. Add corn and green beans and continue cooking until all vegetables are cooked through. Season with salt and pepper.

Slice 1 large heirloom tomato into half-moon shapes. Place one-fourth of the tomatoes on each plate. Spoon succotash onto each plate next to the tomatoes, making sure to leave space for the corn puree. Ladle corn puree next to succotash. Place crispy chicken breast on top of succotash and garnish with Bleu Mont cheddar cheese (you could substitute a good Parmesan here).

Arugula and Walnut Pesto

From Brian Millman of Uncommon Ground

Makes 1 2/3 c. of pesto

4 oz. arugula
3 garlic cloves, minced
1/3 c. toasted walnuts
1/3 c. Parmesan cheese, grated
1/2 tsp. salt
1/4 tsp. black pepper
4 oz. oil

Combine arugula, garlic, and walnuts in food processor and chop until the arugula is broken down. Add Parmesan cheese, salt, and pepper and continue to process until fully incorporated. With food processor running, slowly drizzle in oil until all the oil is added.

Farm Vegetable Pasta Salad
with Arugula and Walnut Pesto

From Brian Millman of Uncommon Ground

Makes 3 c. of pasta salad

2 c. cooked pasta (your choice of pasta)
1/2–1 c. of Arugula and Walnut Pesto
 (see above recipe)
2 oz. green beans, blanched
2 oz. cherry tomatoes
2 oz. carrots, sliced
2 oz. onions, sliced
Shredded Parmesan cheese, as needed

Cook desired pasta and reserve about 1/2 c. of the cooking liquid. Cool pasta completely. In a mixing bowl, combine all ingredients except Parmesan cheese, starting with 1/2 c. of the pesto. The amount of pesto you will need to use will depending on how flavorful the arugula is in the pesto. Taste the pasta salad and determine if you need to add more pesto. If the pesto is too thick and does not coat the pasta, add a small amount of the cooking liquid to thin the pasta salad. Top with shredded Parmesan cheese.

Mint Tzatziki

From Brian Millman of Uncommon Ground

Makes about 2 c. of sauce

2 32-oz. containers good-quality plain yogurt, drained
3 seedless cucumbers, peeled and grated
1/2 tsp. salt
Pinch of white pepper
1/2 tsp. minced garlic
2 tbsp. fresh mint, chopped
1/2 tbsp. lemon juice

Drain yogurt in a colander lined with cheesecloth or a coffee filter in the refrigerator for at least two hours, preferably overnight. Shred cucumber with a box grater over medium-sized holes. Place in a colander set over a bowl in the refrigerator and let drain overnight.

Combine strained cucumber and yogurt. Add the remaining ingredients and whisk together. Check seasoning and add salt and pepper as needed.

Bacon-braised Kale

From Brian Millman of Uncommon Ground

Serves 8

1/2 lb. bacon, sliced
1 yellow onion, diced
2 tbsp. minced garlic
2 lb. kale, washed and cleaned
2 qt. chicken stock
1 lb. butter, cut into small pieces
Salt and pepper, to taste

Brown bacon in stock pot and add onion and garlic. Sweat until softened. Add kale, chicken stock, and butter. Simmer until kale is tender. Season with salt and pepper.

Café at Wild Things

Chef Ron Krivosik

Organic Prairie

Families don't typically go to the zoo expecting high-quality food. It's generally pretty basic fast-food fare.

But the Café at Wild Things at Lincoln Park Zoo is trying to change that.

The café, which overlooks the zoo's lion habitat, serves a menu full of organic, locally sourced, family-friendly, fast-casual foods.

"As a chef, you always look at getting the best flavors out there," says Ron Krivosik, a regional chef for Levy Restaurants, which oversees food at the zoo, as well as all of the major sports facilities in the Chicago area. Levy runs the food operations at more than 100 locations around the United States and Canada. "People want to know their food is safe and where it came from."

Levy has handled food at the Lincoln Park Zoo, located a short walk from the city's Green City Market, for a quarter century. But a few years ago, Krivosik and others began thinking about how to amp up the offerings a bit.

"We said, 'We should look at something totally organic,'" Krivosik says. "It's just what the whole theme of the zoo is about. Now the public, I believe, is more passionate and more insightful about 'Where did my food come from? How was it raised? How was it grown?'"

Krivosik has worked with Levy since 1981. In 1990, he took over food operations at Arlington Park Racetrack in the Chicago suburb of Arlington Heights. While there, he began using produce from local farms.

"From the earth to the table, that's what it's about," he says. "That's how we used to live a hundred years ago. Isn't it crazy how our parents knew exactly what to do?"

Café at Wild Things offers kid-friendly fare such as a warm peanut butter and banana sandwich with honey, macaroni and cheese, and organic hot dogs. For grown-ups (and adventurous kids), there's teriyaki-marinated tofu and a bleu cheese panini with arugula and caramelized onions.

"This is definitely the wave of the future," Krivosik says. "We want to be on the forefront from a company point of view. There's so many people who are so passionate about this in the office. It's an easy sell to everybody."

The zoo café gets much of its protein products—turkey, beef, and hot dogs—from Organic Prairie, an independent cooperative of more than 150 farms that raise organic meat. Organic Prairie is part of Organic Valley, a cooperative of some 1,600 growers around the country.

One of those Organic Prairie farmers is Fred Pedretti, who farms 360 acres outside Genoa, Wisconsin. The land has been in Pedretti's family for years; he and his son Jason are the fourth and fifth generations to farm there, according to information provided by Organic Prairie.

Fred Pedretti's great-grandmother, Adelaide Pedretti, began the farm in 1869, after her husband was killed hauling cordwood. The land has been in the family ever since.

Previous generations focused on milking cows. But higher costs and lower profits forced Fred Pedretti to change what the farm was doing. In 1996, he sold his herd of milking cows. He started growing organic crops in 1999 and began raising organic beef cattle in 2002.

Beef and Bleu Cheese Wrap

From Ron Krivosik of Café at Wild Things

Serves 2

2 oz. red onion, sliced	Salt and pepper, to taste
2 tsp. olive oil	6 oz. Organic Prairie beef steak
2 tbsp. sugar	1 12-in. tortilla
4 oz. balsamic vinegar	1 Roma tomato, chopped
2 oz. bleu cheese	1/2 cup spring mix greens
2 c. mayonnaise	

Saute sliced onion with olive oil. Add sugar and heat until caramelized. Add balsamic vinegar and reduce until thickened, about 2 minutes.

Add the bleu cheese to the mayonnaise, season with salt and pepper.

Season the beef with salt and pepper. Grill or sauté the beef to desired doneness. Cool. Slice 1/2-in. thick.

Warm tortilla in microwave for 10 seconds. Spread blue cheese mayo over tortilla. Top with steak, tomato, spring mix, and onions. Wrap into a long, skinny burrito shape and cut in half.

Turkey Club Panini

From Ron Krivosik of Cafe at Wild Things

Serves 2

4 tbsp. rosemary, chopped
4 tbsp. thyme, chopped
1/2 c. mayonnaise
Salt and pepper, to taste
4 slices rustic bread
2 tbsp. neutral oil
4 oz. white cheddar cheese, sliced
4 oz. Organic Prairie turkey
4 slices good-quality bacon, cooked
2 oz. sliced tomato

Preheat a panini machine or griddle.

Add rosemary and thyme to mayonnaise, season with salt and pepper.

Brush one side of both pieces of bread with neutral oil. On the other side, spread with the herb mayo. Put cheese on one side of the bread. Top with turkey, bacon, and tomato. Cover with the other piece of bread. Place sandwich in panini press or on griddle until golden brown, flipping if necessary. Cut sandwich in half and serve.

fall

Tiptoeing in after the bounty of summer, fall can seem like a thief. But autumn does not steal summer's abundance; it kindly replaces it with luscious roasted acorn squash and tart apple pie and comforting, soul-satisfy spiced soups. Fall is first-day-of-school and cozy new sweater. Fall is gather-round-the-table time. So, join in.

Braised Lamb Leg Osso Bucco
with English Minted Pea Risotto

From Sean Sanders of Browntrout

Serves 4

Neutral cooking oil, as needed
4 pieces of lamb leg, bone-in, cut in 1 1/4-in. pieces
2 c. red wine
2 qt. lamb stock
1 lb. baby carrots
Salt and pepper, to taste

Tie the lamb around its widest part for even cooking. Heat a large pan over medium-high heat. Add oil to cover bottom. Sear lamb legs on all sides until browned. Set aside. In a braising pot, reduce the red wine by half. Add the lamb stock. Bring to a simmer, add the lamb, and cook until the lamb is tender (about 2 hours.) Cool in the liquid.

Skim the fat off the cooled braising liquid. Reduce the liquid over medium heat to make a spoonable sauce, finish with a pat of butter and season to taste.

Boil the baby carrots until tender. Season with salt and pepper. Add lamb to reduced sauce and warm thoroughly until tender. Serve lamb with the sauce, carrots, and Minted English Pea Risotto (recipe follows).

Minted English Pea Risotto

1/2 onion, diced
4 oz. plus 2 oz. butter
1 c. arborio rice
4 oz. white wine
Chicken or vegetable stock, as needed, about 8 c. (all risottos will take a different amount of liquid)
1 c. fresh English peas
3 oz. Parmesan cheese
8 sprigs of mint, julienned
Salt and pepper, to taste

In a large pot, sweat the onion in 4 oz. of butter. Add the rice. Cook until translucent. Add the white wine and cook until it is almost completely absorbed. Start by adding 1/2 c. of stock to the rice, stirring with a wooden spoon. When the stock is absorbed, add another 1/2 cup of stock. Be sure to stir with a wooden spoon so you don't break the grains of rice and release the starch. Continue adding stock, a bit at a time, stirring constantly. The risotto will continue to cook and soften, a process that takes about 30 minutes. About 5 minutes before the rice is done, add the fresh peas and cook for a couple of minutes. Add the Parmesan, 2 oz. butter, and mint. Season with salt and pepper. Serve with the lamb.

Gourmet Gorilla

Chef Danielle Hrzic

Cob Connection

Children might not be into white-tablecloth fussiness or gourmet fare. And most probably they don't care whether they're eating locally grown foods or organic ingredients.

But that doesn't mean they don't deserve to eat school lunches that conform to those high standards. (Well, maybe without the white tablecloths.)

That was the thinking of Danielle Hrzic and her husband, Jason Weedon, who launched Gourmet Gorilla in 2008. The small Chicago company produces largely local, organic lunches for children in schools around the city. In 2010, they served hot lunches to about two dozen schools and cold, boxed lunches to about thirty schools, for a total of 800 students.

Gourmet Gorilla was born after the couple was horrified to see what kind of food their son was being served at preschool. "The fact that the teachers weren't even eating the food was disturbing," Hrzic says. But the school's owners were open to changing the food program, she says, and business grew from there.

The meals are healthy, but still plenty kid-friendly—from cheese tortellini to chicken pot pie to pizza. Vegetable side dishes include glazed carrots, sautéed kale, and roasted broccoli.

"You have to weave in the familiar foods," Hrzic says. "If they're not eating at all, there's no point in serving them."

Gourmet Gorilla gets its local ingredients from several sources, including Cob Connection, a nonprofit organization that employs previously incarcerated adults to grow food at several mini-farms around Chicago.

"Building community food systems. That's what we do," says Chad Bliss, the group's founder and executive director. And he adds that businesses like Gourmet Gorilla are "important in this whole equation." "We're about building relationships; the food just happens to be there."

In the past year, Cob Connection has had sixty-five people go through its yearlong training program. They've learned micro-enterprise skills, and they've learned about production and distribution.

"From seed to market and back," Bliss says.

Those in the program grow carrots, beets, kale, chard, and microgreens for Gourmet Gorilla, as well as other produce for area restaurants and for the group's community supported agriculture (CSA) program.

Bliss likes to ask people in his program what they did the day before they signed on with Cob Connection. Some admit they sold drugs.

"You sold drugs because you had to," he says. "Now, they can start hustling produce; that's what they can do.

"For me, it's about rebuilding communities. That's why this is so important. They come from these communities where they have nothing so they think like nothing. They can take this vacant lot and create a world of abundance instead of a world of lack."

Sweet Apple Chicken Curry
with Jasmine Rice

From Danielle Hrzic of Gourmet Gorilla

1 Amish chicken, about 3 1/2 lb., cut into serving pieces

Salt and pepper, to taste

2 tbsp. olive oil

3 tbsp. unsalted butter, divided

2 ribs of celery, chopped fine

1 large onion, chopped fine

2 garlic cloves, minced

2 Granny Smith apples, cored and chopped

1 bell pepper, chopped

1 tbsp. curry powder

1/2 tsp. cinnamon

1/2 tsp. cumin

2 tbsp. all-purpose flour

2 c. chicken broth

2 tbsp. chopped parsley

Season chicken with salt and pepper and sear in olive oil. Remove chicken and set aside. Add 2 tbsp. of butter. Cook celery, onion, and garlic over moderately low heat, stirring occasionally, until vegetables are softened. Core and chop the apples. Add the apples and cook the mixture, stirring occasionally, for 5 minutes. Add the bell pepper, curry powder, cinnamon, and cumin. Cook the mixture, stirring for an additional minute. Add flour and cook the mixture over moderate heat. Add broth and chicken with any juices that have accumulated. Cover, bring liquid to a boil, and simmer for 15–20 minutes, or until the chicken is tender and cooked through.

Transfer the chicken, with a slotted spoon, to a serving plate. Boil the vegetable mixture, stirring, for 3–5 minutes, or until it is thickened slightly, and season the sauce with salt and pepper. Pour the sauce over the chicken and top with chopped parsley. Serve the curry with steamed Jasmine rice and chutney.

HotChocolate

Chef Mindy Segal
Heritage Prairie Farm

Mindy Segal may be one of the country's most celebrated pastry chefs. But that's not how she thinks of herself.

"I have my own style," Segal says from her popular Chicago restaurant, HotChocolate. "I think of myself as a cook. I don't approach pastry as a pastry chef."

However she approaches her food, it works. She has received four nominations from the prestigious James Beard Foundation for Outstanding Pastry Chef. *Chicago Magazine* and *Time Out Chicago* have hailed her as the city's best pastry chef multiple times.

Segal is driven, with a résumé to prove it. She graduated from Chicago's prestigious Kendall College (in culinary, not pastry) and has worked in some of the country's most well-known kitchens, including Charlie Trotter's and Spago.

She started going to farmers' markets in the mid-1990s while working for Chef Erwin Drechsler's gourmet to-go restaurant, Metropolis.

"He kind of introduced me to this whole local flair," she says. "I liked the relationship you could develop with the farmers. I started thinking this was how I wanted to cook: organic, fresh, local, and seasonal. That's what we do here."

As a child, Segal would watch Julia Child and *The Frugal Gourmet* on TV. She starting cooking from Child's books, throwing baby vegetables and fresh herbs in her dishes and taking a simple oatmeal cookie dough recipe and making it her own.

"There's an innate ability for me to do this," Segal says. "I just knew I had a talent."

When she opened HotChocolate in 2005, she envisioned a dessert bar that served food. Over the years, Segal's upscale comfort cuisine has become just as well known for the savory side of the menu as for the desserts.

"I never thought the food at this restaurant would be what it is now," she admits.

And part of her success comes from sourcing high-quality, locally grown ingredients and using them in creative ways based on classic techniques. (Her inventive chocolate-beet layer cake with honey–cream cheese buttercream, candied beets, and honeycomb candy is a prime example.)

She met the growers of Heritage Prairie Farm at the farmers' market and now uses a variety of their products, including honey, mixed greens, beets, and turnips.

Heritage Prairie Farm grew out of owner Bronwyn Weaver's love of beekeeping. She began bottling and selling her honey on the farm. As business became more successful, she and her husband, Bob Archibald, expanded to cultivate naturally grown produce on 8 acres.

The growing is now managed by Ted Richter, a former fly-fishing guide in Oregon who grew up on a farm in Downer's Grove, Illinois.

"Both my folks were falconers, involved in the reintroduction of peregrines to the Midwest," Richter says. "I've pretty much spent my life outside. I haven't done well with the desk-job program."

Richter earned a degree in political science and considered becoming a lawyer, but knew that wasn't for him. He returned to the Chicago area from Oregon and leased some land from a large farm that was in his family. He began growing heirloom tomatoes and selling them to area restaurants and farmers' markets.

It was a steep learning curve on his one-man farm, Richter says, but he appreciates all he learned now that he manages the growing at Heritage Prairie.

"It is very fulfilling," he says. "Before I came over here, I did absolutely everything on my own. You figure out how to make things work. I ran three markets, sometimes four, and I did it all by myself, with my dog."

Heritage Prairie is based on a model created by Eliot Coleman, a pioneer in organic agriculture.

"I certainly did not move back here and say, 'I'm going to return to my roots,'" Richter says. "I came back here and said, 'How is it I can actually feel good about sleeping during the night?' It was deep during the depth of my discontent with the political system. It seemed like we were headed in the wrong direction."

The farm now has a thriving business selling to restaurants and hotels, along with a CSA and a honey program that allows chefs to purchase their own beehive.

"This place just keeps growing and growing and growing," Richter says.

Even though he is busy supervising activities on the farm, Richter makes a point to work at the farmers' market in Geneva, Illinois, every week.

"You just don't want to be alienated from your product and where it goes," he says. "Or else, you're just screwing on a chassis on a car."

Chocolate Beet Cake

with Cream Cheese Frosting, Candied
Beets Cooked in Raspberry Syrup,
and Honeycomb

From Mindy Segal of HotChocolate

Yields 2 8-in. round or square cakes

RASPBERRY SYRUP AND CANDIED BEETS

2 pt. raspberries
1/2 c. granulated sugar
1 large red beet, very finely diced, reserved

Sprinkle raspberries with sugar. Macerate for 1 hour. Put macerated raspberries and their juices into a pot and cook over medium heat until raspberries break down. Strain liquid and reserve for candied beets. Reserve raspberry pulp for the beet cake.

Place raspberry syrup and diced beets in a small, heavy pot. Bring to a boil. Simmer and cook until beets are tender. If liquid reduces too much, add a little water to thin. Remove from heat and cool. Reserve for serving.

CHOCOLATE BEET CAKE

1 lb. red beets
Raspberry pulp, reserved from recipe above
1 3/4 c. all-purpose flour
1 1/2 tsp. baking soda
1 1/2 tsp. kosher salt
1 c. cane sugar
1/2 c. dark brown sugar
1 c. vegetable or canola oil
3 eggs
1 tsp. vanilla extract
1 oz. unsweetened chocolate, melted

Roast beets in 400°F oven until tender, about 45 minutes. Peel skin from beets and puree with reserved raspberry pulp. Reduce oven temperature to 350°F.

Whisk flour, baking soda, and salt in a bowl and set aside. Combine sugars and oil in the bowl of an electric mixer fitted with a paddle attachment. Add eggs and vanilla, scraping bowl to combine. Add beets and beet juice. While mixing, add flour mixture and chocolate. Scrape sides of bowl to combine. Mix until incorporated.

Spray baking pans generously with cooking oil spray, line with parchment paper, and spray again. Divide batter in half and pour into 8-in. round or square cake pans. Bake until cakes are firm to touch, about 35–40 minutes. Cool completely.

CREAM CHEESE FROSTING

2 lb. butter, room temperature
2 lb. cream cheese, softened
1 lb. powdered sugar, sifted
1 tsp. vanilla
1 tbsp. salt
1 tbsp. honey, or to taste
8 oz. white chocolate, melted

In an electric mixer with paddle attachment, cream butter until smooth. Add cream cheese and beat on medium until smooth, scraping sides of bowl to blend. Add sugar, vanilla, salt, and honey. Beat until smooth. Taste to adjust flavor. Add white chocolate and reserve frosting until you're ready to frost the cake.

HONEYCOMB

3/4 c. granulated sugar
1/4 c. water
1 tbsp. plus 2 tsp. corn syrup
1 1/2 tbsp. Heritage Prairie Farm honey
1/2 tsp. kosher salt
1/2 tsp. baking powder

Place sugar, water, corn syrup, honey, and salt in a large, heavy saucepan. Combine thoroughly, cook over high heat until mixture starts to caramelize around the edges. Stir together to form an even color. When the sugar is light caramel-colored, remove from heat. Add baking powder. Mixture will foam and quadruple in volume. Mix quickly. Adjust taste with sugar if needed. Pour onto an oiled sheet pan and cool. Once cool, break into shards.

Once the cake has cooled, remove from pans. Line 1 cake pan with plastic wrap. Invert one of the cakes into the plastic-wrapped cake pan and spread frosting about 1/3 in. thick. Invert other cake over the top. Cover with plastic. Refrigerate until set, about 2 hours. Remove cake from pan and invert so the bottom becomes the top. Place on a plate or cake round and frost as desired with cream cheese frosting. Serve each slice of cake with a sprinkle of candied beets and a shard of honeycomb.

The Butcher
& Larder

Chefs Rob and Allie Levitt

Spence Farm

Rob Levitt didn't set out to become a chef.

He went to college to study jazz saxophone, which naturally led to a job washing dishes in Urbana, Illinois. Pretty soon, he took a job as a prep cook there.

"I started washing dishes and just thought being in the kitchen was really cool," he says.

It wasn't long before he'd traded his sax for a spot at the Culinary Institute of America in New York. While there, he met Allie, the woman who would become his wife. She worked at the famed Gramercy Tavern. The two would spend their days off together, shopping farmers' markets and preparing meals.

"We would walk around and find fun stuff," Rob says. "I'd get a chicken. Allie would get fruit and cheese and we'd put together dinner that night. It was always these very simple meals."

The two had grown weary of "fine-dining" restaurants.

"Just sick of going to different restaurants and doing the same thing," Rob says. "The attitude, the rituals. Everything that was involved in going to a 'good' restaurant, we never have any fun. We like to be goofy and have fun and listen to music. And make really good food."

And in April 2008, Mado (which takes its name from the hard-working wife of a French restaurater) was born. Little more than a year later, *Bon Appetit* magazine named it one of the ten best new restaurants in the country, calling the Levitts "fanatical about local and sustainable ingredients."

On Halloween 2010, the Levitts announced they would leave Mado to open Chicago's first whole-animal butcher shop, The Butcher & Larder. But they're certainly not leaving behind their farm-to-table approach.

The shop offers custom-cut meats from animals raised on small Midwestern farms, along with a daily assortment of sausages, pates and other specialty items. The Levitts also serve a lunch menu of sandwiches, soups, and charcuterie, all based on farm-fresh ingredients. The Butcher & Larder hosts occasional butchering and charcuterie classes and sells sausages and other meat products to a handful of Chicago restaurants.

The Mado crew made regular visits to Chicago's Green City Market to source produce and meat from a variety of local growers. But Rob Levitt has had a long relationship with Spence Farm, one that started years ago when he was a sous chef at another restaurant.

The operation at Spence Farm is also a family affair, one that has been ongoing for seven generations. The 160-acre farm in Fairbury, Illinois, gained notoriety with Chicago-area restaurants several years ago by selling wild ramps to a handful of chefs.

And that's just how Rob met Marty and Kris Spence, when a group of chefs were invited to the farm one early spring day to dig ramps and learn how they are grown.

"At first I was just seeing Marty during ramp season. Pretty soon he was stopping by every Wednesday," Rob says.

Now, the Levitts buy a variety of things from Spence Farm to use at Mado—maple syrup, Swiss chard, fava beans, cranberry beans, wheat berries, and even cattail shoots.

"I'll say, 'Marty, what the heck is a cattail shoot?' And Marty will tell you what to do," Rob says.

Every Friday, Marty Spence e-mails about fifty Chicago chefs, letting them know what he has available.

"I've come to realize the chefs don't know what they want," he says. "It's just, 'What've you got?' We'll deal with it."

The Spence family does not simply consider farming a way to make a living. They think of themselves as stewards of the land, entrusted to keep the farm thriving for seven more generations, all the while preserving heirloom varieties of produce.

At a dinner at Mado in spring 2009 featuring Spence Farm produce, guests raved about the cornbread, made with the farm's Iroquois white corn. But the story behind the corn, as told by Spence, might be even more jaw-dropping.

Several years ago, Chef Rick Bayless of Frontera Grill in Chicago called Spence Farm, asking if they could grow Iroquois white corn for cornmeal.

Spence searched the country for the corn seed with no luck. Finally, he found a Canadian company selling the seed at $50 per pound. Spence Farms bought a pound and a half, enough for eight rows of corn in 2007. From that corn, they saved 9 pounds of prime seed to plant the following year. They roasted and milled the remaining 63 pounds and sent it to Frontera.

The family bought an additional five pounds of seed from Canada and continue to see growing harvests of Iroquois white corn, always careful to reserve seed and save it from extinction.

Spence Farm also grows a bean that has been handed down through the family for generations. The Kickapoo bean was given to Spence's fourth great-grandfather by the Native American tribe.

"Small family farms are alive," he says. "It's a challenge, and it's going to continue to be a challenge. There's not enough small family farms. Part of our mission is to continue to raise the awareness and create the demand."

Crostone of German Howard Tomato Conserva

with Zucchini Agro-Dolce

From Chef Rob Levitt of The Butcher & Larder

TOMATO CONSERVA

- **2 cloves garlic, peeled**
- **2 sprigs fresh thyme**
- **3 tbsp. olive oil**
- **10 German Howard tomatoes, coarsely chopped**
- **Salt, to taste**

Place garlic, thyme, and olive oil in a large, heavy pan over medium heat. When the oil is hot and the garlic is just beginning to sizzle, add the chopped tomatoes. Cook for about 10 minutes, or until the tomatoes are broken down and just starting to color. Pass through the small holes of a food mill and return to the pan. Cook gently over low heat until it's almost as thick as tomato paste. Let cool. Season to taste with salt. Tomato conserva can be stored for about two weeks in a container, topped with a layer of olive oil to help preserve it.

ZUCCHINI AGRO-DOLCE

- **4 large zucchini**
- **2 tbsp. fresh marjoram**
- **1/4 c. plus 2 tbsp. extra-virgin olive oil**
- **Salt and pepper, to taste**
- **1/4 c. red wine vinegar**
- **3 tbsp. sugar**

Slice the zucchini as thinly as possible, either with a sharp knife or mandoline. Toss the zucchini slices with marjoram, 2 tbsp. olive oil, and a bit of salt and pepper. Cook on a medium grill or in a relatively hot pan until just wilted, but still with a bit of bite left in them. Remove zucchini to a mixing bowl. Whisk together vinegar, sugar, and remaining olive oil and pour over zucchini. Toss and season to taste with salt and pepper. Zucchini can be made up to two days in advance and benefit from extra time marinating. Bring the zucchini and conserva to room temperature. Toast some bread on the grill or in the oven or toaster. Cut a big slice per guest and, while still hot, rub one side with a clove of peeled garlic. Spread a generous layer of conserva over the bread and top with a mound of marinated zucchini.

Roasted Acorn Squash, Apple, and Chestnut Salad

From Chef Rob Levitt
of The Butcher & Larder

2 tbsp. apple cider

1/4 c. apple cider vinegar

Salt and pepper, to taste

1/2 c. extra-virgin olive oil plus 3 tbsp. more for cooking

2 sage leaves

1 small sprig rosemary

1 acorn squash, cut into 1/2-in. wedges

1/4 lb. chestnuts, roasted and peeled

3 apples

1/4 lb. baby arugula

Combine apple cider, cider vinegar, salt, pepper, and 1/2 c. olive oil in a container with a tight seal and shake vigorously.

Heat 3 tbsp. of olive oil in a pan large enough to hold squash pieces in one layer. When oil is very hot, add sage and rosemary. Add squash and cook until golden brown. Turn squash, lower heat to medium, and cover pan. Cook until just tender and allow to cool to room temperature.

Slice peeled chestnuts and apples and combine in mixing bowl with arugula and squash. Season with salt and pepper and dress with apple cider vinaigrette.

Tuscan Faro and Cranberry Bean Soup

From Chef Rob Levitt
of The Butcher & Larder

1 c. cranberry beans, shelled

3 cloves garlic

1 sprig rosemary

1 c. faro (Spence Farm wheat berries)

3 tbsp. olive oil

10 sage leaves

1 medium onion, diced

1 large carrot, cut into thin half circles

1 German Howard tomato, peeled and finely chopped

Salt and pepper, to taste

Place the beans, garlic, and rosemary in a heavy-bottomed pot. Cover with water by 2 in. and cook on low heat until tender, about 20–30 minutes. Remove the rosemary, but leave beans in cooking liquid until needed. This can be done up to one day ahead, but return beans to room temperature before finishing the soup.

Spread the wheat berries on a baking sheet and toast in a 375°F oven for 5 minutes, until fragrant. Heat the olive oil in a heavy-bottomed pot over medium heat. Add half of the sage leaves. Once the oil is fragrant with the sage, add the onion and carrot and cook until softened. Add the chopped tomato and cook, stirring frequently, until the tomato is broken down and beginning to caramelize. Season with salt and pepper and add the wheat berries. Stir and add enough water to cover. Simmer until the wheat berries are very tender, and just starting to split.

Place two-thirds of the cooked wheat berries and two-thirds of the cooked cranberry beans in a blender. Blend with just enough of the bean cooking liquid to form a smooth puree, about the thickness of heavy cream. When ready to serve, reheat the puree and add the remaining beans and wheat berries. Season with salt and pepper. If desired, fry the remaining sage leaves in a little bit of olive oil. Serve the soup in warm bowls garnished with the fried sage and the perfumed oil, or with just a drizzle of your best-quality extra-virgin olive oil.

Spence Farm Cornbread

From Spence Farm, adapted from
"The Tasha Tudor Cookbook"

1 stick of butter

2/3 c. sugar

2 farm-fresh eggs, separated and at room temperature

1 c. Spence Farm whole-wheat flour

3 tsp. baking powder

1/4 tsp. salt

1 c. milk, lukewarm

1 c. Spence Farm roasted Iroquois white cornmeal

Preheat oven to 400°F. Grease an iron skillet with oil.

In large mixing bowl, cream the butter and sugar, add the egg yolks, slightly beaten. Stir well.

In another bowl, beat the egg whites until stiff. Mix the flour with the baking powder and salt. Add it alternately with the milk into the creamed butter. Stir in the cornmeal and fold in the egg whites. Pour into the skillet and bake for 25 minutes. Serve with honey or maple syrup.

Nightwood and Lula Cafe

Chefs Jason Hammel and Amalea Tshilds
City Farm

Jason Hammel and his wife, Amalea Tshilds, had no formal culinary training when they opened their wildly popular Lula Cafe in 1999.

But they've received a graduate-level education in restaurant ownership in the years since and have recently expanded, debuting the upscale, farm-to-table Nightwood restaurant in the Pilsen neighborhood on Chicago's South Side.

Hammel and Tshilds actually met at Lula, back before it was Lula, when it was still a neighborhood coffee shop. "The cafe closed and we bought it," Hammel says.

The couple didn't set out to become a landing spot for so much locally grown produce, but it didn't take long, since the couple frequented farmers' markets themselves.

"It developed pretty quickly," Hammel says. "We had farmers showing up pretty quickly after we started going to the markets. It became important because we were concerned with quality. We never set out to market ourselves in that sense (as a farm-to-table restaurant). We never set out to create something that had a marketable commodity. We just wanted good vegetables, so we started going to the market ourselves."

Lula Cafe features a casual and inventive diner-style menu that's not completely local since regular customers demand the same favorites year-round. But Hammel and Tshilds' latest restaurant, Nightwood, relies on entirely locally sourced products, Hammel says.

"We wanted to a 100 percent farm-to-table concept," he says. "We wanted to open a restaurant from the ground up. We wanted to give the staff, who was with us for a long time, the opportunity to do their own thing."

But, Hammel admits, "It's really hard to make a farm-to-table concept work in Chicago. It's really difficult to pay the kind of top-dollar amounts and give the kind of Midwest portions people expect." And yet he remains committed because of the quality, and for less tangible reasons.

"Part of the reason for doing what we do is the interpersonal relationships we have with the people who grow our stuff," Hammel says. "I feel like my life is very rich. It's amazing I get to do this every day and talk to these people and know what I know about food and the local economy. I know that we're really busy, so I know people are interested in what we're doing."

Hammel and Tshilds have developed relationships with a number of farmers over the years. They've worked with City Farm, a Chicago urban-agriculture project, since about 2003, when it began. They've even seen a couple of their cooks from Lula go on to work with the farm.

Andy Rozendaal started as director of urban agriculture with City Farm in April 2010. The job is a perfect fit for his skills and interests. Rozendaal grew up on a farm in Iowa, attended Iowa State University to study agriculture, and then went on to become an associate minister.

"I wanted to put my two backgrounds together," Rozendaal says.

The 1-acre City Farm is near Chicago's tony Gold Coast, but it also abuts the site of the former Cabrini-Green housing project, one of the roughest neighborhoods in the city. City Farm is run by the Resource Center, a nonprofit recycle and reuse organization.

City Farm is looking at other plots of unused land around Chicago to expand its reach, Rozendaal says. "We can use the land and use a wasted space and turn it into something useful, to provide a place of green and nature," he says. "We can feed a lot of people. We want to educate people about sustainable opportunities. People don't know where their food comes from."

Hundreds of volunteers help each year with work on the farm. "They can plant a seed and watch it grow and come back later in the year to harvest it," Rozendaal says. The farm sells more than eighty varieties of vegetables and gets about 60 to 75 percent of its revenue from restaurant buyers.

City Farm is starting a small CSA, and Rozendaal would eventually like to see a percentage of those shares given away to people in need who live near the farm. He also hopes the farm can run cooking classes to teach people what to do with the produce.

"I wanted to sweat and I wanted to do something," he says. "I didn't want to sit behind a desk all day long. I'm really looking forward to true community development."

Overwintered Parsnip Soup

with Toasted Almond Saltine, Fresh Herbs, and Crème Fraîche

From Jason Hammel of Nightwood

Serves 6

1 tbsp. allspice

1 tbsp. fennel

1 tbsp. anise

3 tbsp. coriander

1/2 c. honey

2 whole, pitted dates

1/3 c. butter, plus 3 tbsp. cold butter, divided

6 leeks, diced, tops reserved

2 c. vermouth

2 lb. parsnips, chopped

2 garlic cloves, sliced

1 small bunch parsley

1 bunch savory

1 bulb fennel

Vegetable or chicken stock, to cover

Salt, to taste

1 tbsp. champagne or cider vinegar

1 c. mixed fresh herbs

1/4 c. crème fraîche

Make a spice blend by combining allspice, fennel, anise, and coriander in a dry pan over medium heat until fragrant. Grind in a spice or coffee grinder. (Extra spice blend is great on grilled fish, pork, or other meats.)

Heat a heavy-bottomed stock pot over medium and add honey. Caramelize with the whole dates until nearly burning, very dark and fragrant. Immediately add butter and 1 tbsp. of spice mix, along with the diced leeks. Sweat at least an hour, over low heat.

Deglaze the pot with vermouth, cook until dry. Add parsnips, garlic cloves, and a cheesecloth filled and tied (bouquet garni) with leek tops, parsley, savory, and fennel. Cover the mixture completely with vegetable or chicken stock and simmer until the parsnips are very tender.

Cool. Remove the filled cheesecloth. Blend in batches on high in a blender or in the pot with an immersion blender, until smooth and luscious. Pass soup through a fine-mesh strainer. Season with salt and a splash of champagne or cider vinegar.

SALTINES

3 1/2 c. all-purpose flour

1 tbsp. baking powder

1/2 c. toasted almonds, ground with 1 tbsp. spice mix (see recipe above)

1/3 c. butter, super-cold and diced small

Milk, as needed, roughly 1 c.

3 tbsp. olive oil

Coarse salt, to taste

Combine flour, baking powder, and almond mixture. Add butter, cut in as for biscuits with two knives or your fingers. Add in enough milk so the dough comes together and forms a ball. On parchment, roll dough to 1/4-in. thickness, letting it rest a few minutes if it shrinks back. Brush dough with olive oil, sprinkle with coarse salt, and bake in a 300°F oven until golden brown.

ALMOND OIL

1 c. whole almonds

Inexpensive olive oil, to cover

Toast whole almonds gently in 2 tbsp. oil until golden and evenly brown. Remove to a small pot. Cover with oil and infuse for 4–6 hours at lowest temperature.

To serve: Reheat soup. Add pieces of butter to thicken soup, about 3 tbsp. Crack saltines into soup. Top with a handful of mixed fresh herbs (such as chervil and parsley). Top with a dollop of crème fraîche.

Beets and Mountain Spinach Salad
with Smoked Walleye, Marinated Cheese Curds, Lemon, and Candied Caraway

From Jason Hammel of Nightwood

Serves 6

1 smoked walleye (can also substitute smoked trout or whitefish)

1 lb. red orach, lamb's-quarter, or spinach, washed

2 tbsp. lemon juice

3 tbsp. best-quality olive oil

1 tbsp. fresh dill, chopped

1 tsp. grated horseradish

GOLDEN BEET GASTRIQUE

2 golden beets, juiced

1/2 c. sugar

2 tbsp. malt vinegar

1 gram xanthan gum (or 1 tsp. cornstarch)

Add sugar and malt vinegar to beet juice. Blend with xanthan gum or cornstarch until just slightly thickened.

MARINATED CHEESE CURDS

1/2 c. cheese curds

1 tbsp. fresh dill, chopped

1 tsp. caraway

Zest of 1 lemon

Olive oil, to cover

Marinate cheese in remaining ingredients, covered in the refrigerator, for at least 2 hours.

ROASTED BEETS

4–8 beets, depending on size

1/2 cup olive oil, plus 1 tbsp.

Salt, to taste

1 tbsp. lemon juice

Toss beets in olive oil and salt. Wrap in foil packages and roast at 375°F until fork tender. Remove skin while still warm. Slice in quarters or sixths, depending on size. Slice a flat side on the root end so the beet can stand up on the plate. Toss sliced beets with a splash of lemon juice and good-quality olive oil.

CANDIED CARAWAY

1 c. caraway

1/2 c. white sugar

Combine caraway and sugar in a heavy-bottomed pan until sugar melts and caramelizes, remove from heat and cool. Break into small pieces.

CARAWAY CRACKERS

1 lb., 3 oz. all-purpose flour

1 tsp. salt

1 3/4 oz. cold butter, diced

14 oz. whole milk

1 tbsp. malt vinegar

1 c. caraway seeds, soaked in hot water until bloomy,
  then drained, then cooled

2 tbsp. olive oil

Cut flour, salt, and butter together with two knives or your fingers until the mixture resembles coarse sand. Add milk and vinegar and mix until well combined. Add bloomed caraway seeds. Let dough rest. Roll out to 1/4-in. thickness. Brush with oil and bake at 350°F until golden and crispy.

To serve: Drizzle golden beet sauce around the plate. Stagger beets, standing straight up, around the plate. Sprinkle with marinated cheese curds and pieces of smoked fish. Lean crackers against the beets. Place greens on top of crackers. Sprinkle platter with dill, fresh-grated horseradish, and candied caraway seeds.

North Pond

Chef Bruce Sherman
Genesis Growers

Vicki Westerhoff took to farming out of necessity.

She'd been diagnosed with chronic fatigue syndrome and the Epstein-Barr virus in 1991. Some days she was so exhausted she'd sleep for twenty hours and still feel horrible during her rare waking moments.

Worn out and miserable, she decided a change in diet would rejuvenate her. When she couldn't find organic produce in the stores in her small town near Kankakee, Illinois, she realized she'd have to grow her own—an impressive feat for someone who was nearly bedridden.

"I'm just very tenacious," says Westerhoff, who had been a gardener but had never done any large-scale farming. "And when I did begin, I did start feeling better. At first it was just an inkling. But that inkling was enough of a promise."

Westerhoff's Genesis Growers took root in 1999, farming on just 1 acre of land that had been in her family for years. Even as she started feeling better, she noticed the land itself was not as healthy as it had once been.

"The earthworms were no longer there. There were no longer toads," Westerhoff says. "I ended up with a secondary vision and that was to heal the land. It was kind of a combined thing of healing myself and healing the land."

Genesis Growers now sells produce to some twenty-five chefs in the Chicago area, including Bruce Sherman of North Pond.

Sherman has taken his family and restaurant employees down to visit Westerhoff's farm several times to give them a better sense of where the food comes from.

During these visits, Sherman can see that they get it. "That's really rewarding for me," he explains.

Sherman, the chef at Lincoln Park eatery North Pond since 1999, developed a deep appreciation for seasonal ingredients while living in India during the mid-1990s.

"During my time there, we didn't have the option of deciding what to cook before we went shopping," Sherman says. "It was a matter of what was available. Winter meant going to the vegetable *wallah* [vendor] and finding a limited amount of product that was available. It had a profound impact on how I think about food."

After his time in India, Sherman moved to Paris to study French cuisine.

Once he returned to the States, he brought that local, seasonal approach with him. You won't find too many curries or dals on his menu, but you will find an abundance of foods from local growers—many of whom, like Westerhoff, he has developed relationships with over many years.

"What this is really about is community," Sherman says. "You can't easily patronize farmers and get product without trying to reach out and understand what they do."

Sherman estimates he has visited about 80 percent of the farms from which he gets produce, and he encourages his staff to do the same. He also serves as chairman of the board of Chefs Collaborative, a nonprofit network of chefs working to promote a sustainable food system.

"It's not just about getting a nameless, faceless box of beauty heart radishes at the door," he says. "But it's understanding whose they are. There's a much greater appreciation of the product itself and the work that goes into it."

The son of a banker, Sherman majored in economics at the University of Pennsylvania and studied at the London School of Economics. That first experience abroad opened his eyes to world cuisine, and he later moved to Boston to start a new career in restaurant management. But he longed to be in the kitchen, so he launched a catering business.

Sherman has high standards for the produce he selects. He's not looking for a boutique, heirloom name that looks cool on a menu. Just because the food came from a midwestern farmer doesn't mean it's perfect.

"Sometimes I have a difficult time getting people to understand it's not about the warm and fuzzy," he says. "If it can't stand up to the pan or the taste, I don't want to use it." But, he adds, "Ninety-five percent of the time it tastes better than an industry-grown product."

Westerhoff herself eats a diet almost entirely made up of food she has grown. Her energy has returned to normal, she says. And the land, as well as her business, is thriving. She is now able to employ three year-round workers to tend to the farm.

"I try to emulate what our forebears would've grown to feed their families for one year," she says. "I try to maintain that kind of diversity."

Rosemary-infused Carrots

From Bruce Sherman of North Pond

Serves 4

1 lb. organic carrots, peeled
2 cloves fresh garlic, peeled
2 tbsp. olive oil
Salt and pepper
2 fresh rosemary sprigs
1 tsp. fresh parsley, chopped

Lay the carrots flat on a cutting board and cut them on the diagonal into 1/8-in. ovals. Gently tap the garlic with the side of a knife, just until the flesh cracks.

Heat olive oil over medium-high heat in a large (12-in.) nonstick pan for 1 minute, and then add in the carrots and lightly crushed garlic. Let sit without shaking the pan for 3 minutes.

Sprinkle some salt and pepper over the carrots, place the two rosemary sprigs in the pan, and stir, turning the carrots so the uncooked sides become exposed to the direct heat.

Cook undisturbed for an additional 3 minutes. The carrots will be lightly browned on each side.

Pick out a carrot and taste it for seasoning and doneness. If it's not tender, cook for 1 additional minute.

Finish by sprinkling with the chopped fresh parsley.

Spiced Organic Carrot Soup

From Bruce Sherman of North Pond

Serves 4

1 tbsp. olive oil

1 shallot, peeled and thinly sliced

1 clove of garlic, peeled and chopped

1/2 rib of celery, thinly sliced

1 scant tsp. fresh ginger, peeled and chopped

1 lb. organic carrots, peeled and thinly sliced

1 head of fennel, white bulb part only, cored and thinly sliced

1/2 tsp. coriander powder

3 c. chicken stock or bouillon

2 oz. butter, cut into small cubes

Salt and white pepper

Over a medium flame, heat the olive oil in a saucepan and add in the chopped shallot, garlic, celery, and ginger. Stir for 1–2 minutes, until they soften slightly. (Make sure they have not browned.) Add the chopped carrots and fennel, and a pinch of salt and pepper, and continue to stir for an additional 2–4 minutes, until the carrots and fennel soften, again trying to avoid any browning. When the vegetables are soft, add in the coriander powder and stir for 1 minute. Add in the chicken stock or bouillon and gently bring the mixture to a boil. Turn down heat and gently simmer for 15 minutes, until the carrots and fennel easily mash with gentle pressure.

Remove the mixture from the heat and place in a blender or puree with a handheld blender. Add in the pieces of butter and continue to blend until very smooth, about 2 minutes. If possible, strain the soup through a fine-mesh strainer into a clean pot. Reheat and season to taste with salt and pepper. Set aside in a warm place for the meal.

Double-stuffed Delicata Squash, Cider *Glace*, Fennel-Carrot Slaw, and Halibut

From Bruce Sherman of North Pond

Serves 2–4

DELICATA SQUASH

2 Delicata squash

2 tbsp. canola or vegetable oil

Salt and white pepper

1/2 c. fresh pressed unfiltered apple cider

1/2 c. apple cider vinegar

1/2 c. fresh Parmesan cheese, grated

1/2 c. fresh breadcrumbs

1/4 c. maple syrup

1 large, firm seasonal apple; peeled, cored, and diced in
  1/4-in. pieces

4 oz. fresh goat cheese

1/4 c. toasted pecans, chopped

1 tbsp. unsalted butter, chilled

CIDER *GLACE*

1/4 c. lemon juice

2 tsp. water

1 tsp. honey

1 tsp. whole-grain mustard

1 small garlic clove, peeled and minced

Salt and pepper, to taste

2/3 c. canola/sunflower oil

FENNEL-CARROT SLAW

1 bulb fennel, approximately 10 oz.

2 medium organic carrots, approximately 8 oz.

1 small, mild slicing onion (such as Walla Walla or Granex)

1 lemon, juiced

1 tbsp. chives, chopped

1 tbsp. parsley, chopped

4 5-oz. halibut filets, cooked

Preheat oven to 350°F.

Halve squash from end to end. Oil, salt, and pepper the halves and place on a cookie sheet cut side up. Roast in the oven for 30–40 minutes, until flesh yields easily to touch.

While squash bakes, place cider and cider vinegar in a small nonreactive saucepan on medium heat. Bring to boil, reduce, and simmer until 3 tbsp. syrup remain. Turn off heat, but keep warm. Mix grated cheese and breadcrumbs. Reserve.

Place maple syrup in the hot saucepan, cook over high heat until reduced by half. Add diced apples and toss to coat, cooking 1 minute more. Remove and reserve.

Whisk lemon juice, water, honey, whole-grain mustard, finely minced garlic, salt, and pepper together in small bowl. Gradually add in oil while whisking. Season to taste and reserve.

When the squash is finished roasting, remove from oven and carefully scoop out and discard seeds from central cavity. Next, scoop out flesh, trying to avoid penetrating the skin. Reserve squash hulls.

Place squash flesh in mixing bowl and mix in reserved maple apples, goat cheese, toasted pecans, and 1/4 cup of breadcrumb mixture. Season to taste.

Place the mixture back into the squash hulls, dust liberally with balance of breadcrumb mix, and place back in oven. Bake an additional 15 minutes, until tops are lightly browned.

NOTE: Stuffed squash can be prepared 12–24 hours in advance.

Cut both the peeled onion and the fennel in half through roots and place them flat on cutting board. Using vegetable slicer or very sharp knife, cut each in very thin slices across width of the piece, creating small "crescents." Place them, fully submerged, in bowl of ice water to soak at least 1 hour.

Halve peeled carrots lengthwise, and then slice (or grate) as thinly as possible, either by hand or with the help of a vegetable slicer. Place in mixing bowl.

Strain fennel and onion and place in mixing bowl. Pour in enough prepared dressing to generously coat vegetables, toss in chopped parsley and chives, and season to taste.

Gently heat apple reduction and whisk in butter. To serve, place one squash next to a small pile of salad on each of four plates. Spoon pool of cider glace on plate, place halibut filet atop, and serve.

Province

Chef Randy Zweiban
Becker Lane Organic Farm

Jude Becker's family has been pig farming since 1850. But the last years of the twentieth century saw the family business sinking into the mud. Becker knew he had to make a change.

"People get these ideas that I just picked up where my father left off," he says. "Obviously, my ancestors weren't niche organic artisanal foodie people. I took a business that was running into a wall in the 1990s and reinvented it: What can we do to create pathways between this farm and food artisans?"

He began working with Whole Foods in 2003 and was soon approached by a Japanese company to sell his pork in Asia. Becker flew to Japan and told his story at restaurants and grocery stores. He was thrilled to see the excitement generated by that relationship.

"People really took to that," Becker says. "Why, golly, why not do that right in my backyard?"

He started forging relationships with chefs. Alice Waters and her disciples became fans, and business exploded. Becker was even featured on an episode of *Oprah* in 2008 about ethically raised animals.

"Suddenly, people started calling," he says. "I would characterize what we do as adding the acumen and the aesthetic of the vineyard to the pig yard."

Since 2007, Becker has fed a small number of his pigs a diet of acorns to mimic the prized pork that's raised in Italy and Spain. His pricey "acorn edition" pigs are now scooped up by chefs around the country who love the rich flavor and impressive marbling of the meat.

Thanks to specially designed insulated metal houses, Becker can keep his pigs outside during the winter to ensure year-round production. He harvests 6,000 pigs—Berkshire and Chester White heritage breeds—each year on his 400-acre organic farm.

Becker's father died in 2003, just as the reinvigorated business was starting to take off. But, Becker says, "I think he enjoyed watching all this happen."

Working with chefs and seeing his family name on the menu is "rejuvenating," he says. "It makes you feel like what you're doing matters and has an impact on people. I really want to live in a world that puts value on food and good, genuine human labor, and the kind of economy where there's a local exchange of goods and services and the culture that comes from that. It's 'agriculture' for a reason, not 'agribusiness.'"

Chef Randy Zweiban has cultivated relationships with farmers for most of his culinary career. He has cooked in Chicago since 1998, but spent many years before that working in Miami and Los Angeles.

"The quality of what we get from growers far outweighs what you can get commodity-wise," Zweiban says. "The food I do, some of it is pretty simple. It always has to start out with great ingredients in order to have a great product that's finished."

Zweiban grew up influenced by his Italian mom, who loved cooking and gardening. He originally wanted to be a drummer in a rock band, though, and even spent time as a diamond setter before going to culinary school.

"Growing up in New York, I was definitely influenced by Puerto Rican cuisine and a lot of Central American cuisine and the intermix of Asian and Latin flavors," Zweiban says.

Mangoes, for example are seen in both Thai and Latin dishes, he says. It's the same with chilies and many other foods.

"I've always been enthralled by ingredients from both," he says. "I've always really liked those flavors."

In Chicago, he spent nearly ten years as the head chef of Nuevo Latin hotspot Nacional 27 before opening his own restaurant—Province—in 2009. The restaurant was built with sustainable materials and is filled with environmentally friendly equipment.

"We try to keep our carbon footprint down," Zweiban says. "There's no bottled water and no bottled beer. We only serve sustainable seafood. It's really important for us to know where our food comes from and how it's produced."

Zweiban enjoys cooking with the pork shoulder and belly he buys from Becker Lane Organic Farm. "We've played with different cooking techniques with different products of theirs," he says. "We marinate them. We dry-rub them one day, wet-rub them the next day, and slow-braise them overnight on the third day.

"What farmers do is basically the same thing I do; whether they're growing an animal or growing produce, they're passionate about getting the best possible product when finished."

But, he added, "What (farmers) do is harder than what we do. There's a huge mutual respect on both sides of it."

Pork
Ropa Vieja

Pork Ropa Vieja with Bourbon
BBQ Salsa and Pork Belly Hash

From Randy Zweiban of Province

Serves 6

SPICE RUB
- 1/2 c. whole cumin
- 1/2 c. whole black peppercorns
- 2 tbsp. whole coriander seeds
- 2 tbsp. kosher salt
- 1/4 c. sugar
- 1/4 c. smoked paprika

In a warm, dry sauté pan, toast the cumin, peppercorns, and coriander over moderate heat until the spices begin to let off a small puff of smoke. Let the spices cool in a bowl and then grind in a small coffee grinder. Combine spices with the remaining ingredients.

ORANGE MOJO
- 1 1/2 c. canola oil
- 1 tbsp. fresh garlic, chopped
- 1 serrano chili, diced
- 1 tbsp. toasted ground cumin
- 1 c. orange juice
- 1/4 c. fresh-squeezed lime juice
- 1 tbsp. fresh cilantro, chopped
- 1 tbsp. chives, chopped
- 1/4 c. shallots, diced

Heat the oil in a small pot to 170°F. Make sure it is not boiling. Reduce 1 c. of fresh-squeezed orange juice down to 1/2 c. In a bowl, combine the garlic and serrano chili and pour the warm oil over them. Let the mixture cool to room temperature and add the rest of the ingredients.

PORK
- 5 lb. pork shoulder, trimmed
- 1 c. spice rub (recipe above)
- 3/4 gal. vegetable or pork stock
- 2 c. Orange Mojo (recipe above)

If you have time, rub the pork with spice rub, wrap in plastic, and place in the refrigerator overnight. The next day, soak the pork in stock and mojo overnight. On the third day, cook the pork, covered in foil, at 200°F for 9 hours. To speed cooking time, cut the pork into smaller pieces.

BOURBON BBQ SALSA
- 1 c. fresh-squeezed orange juice
- 1 c. vegetable or pork stock
- 1 tsp. fresh ginger, diced
- 1/2 c. bourbon
- 1/2 c. ketchup
- 1 tbsp. smoked paprika
- 2 tbsp. honey
- 1 1/2 tbsp. molasses
- Toasted and ground black pepper and kosher salt, to taste

Combine the orange juice, stock, and ginger. Reduce by half. In a separate small pot, reduce the bourbon to 1 tbsp. Combine all ingredients and blend in an electric blender. Season with toasted and ground black pepper and kosher salt.

ROPA VIEJA
- 1/2 gal. cooked pork, shredded
- 1 c. poblano peppers, roasted, seeded, peeled, and julienned
- 1 c. onions, julienned and lightly sautéed
- 1 1/4 c. Bourbon BBQ Salsa (recipe above)

Combine all ingredients in a saucepan and heat until warm. Season with toasted and ground black pepper and kosher salt.

PORK BELLY HASH
- 2 tbsp. mayonnaise
- 1/4 tsp. garlic
- 1/4 tsp. jalapeño, chopped
- 1/4 c. canola oil
- 1 c. pork belly, cooked and diced
- 2 1/2 c. green beans, cooked and cut
- 2 1/2 c. corn kernels, blistered
- Ground pepper and kosher salt, to taste

With a mortar and pestle, combine the mayonnaise, garlic, and jalapeño.

In a hot sauté pan, heat the oil and then add the pork belly. When it is slightly rendered, add the green beans, and after a minute, add the corn. Toss the vegetable mix. When it's warm, add the mayonnaise mixture. Season with ground pepper and kosher salt.

Spoon about 3/4 c. of the vegetables in the center of a plate or a bowl. Top with the ropa vieja and garnish with more of the salsa.

The Bristol

Chef Chris Pandel

Hasselmann Family Farm

To watch Chef Chris Pandel butcher a hog is to understand his reverence for his ingredients and the farmers who produce them.

During a dinner-party demonstration in the restaurant's upstairs dining room, he showed the gathered crowd the tenderloin and pointed out that it's but a tiny fraction of the edible parts of the animal. Such a waste, he explained to the group, to buy only that one small portion. Pandel, chef of Chicago's acclaimed restaurant The Bristol, goes whole-hog, like a growing number of Chicago chefs, using every part of the animal in his dishes, even the head.

"I'm a big believer in 'come say hi to your food,'" Pandel says. "The ingredients are always the first thing. We use the whole animal and use local foods because we can. We have little to no waste. People think it's adventurous eating, but it's just eating."

Pandel got his start at the Chew Chew Cafe in his hometown of Riverside, Illinois, where a job painting chairs and hanging awnings ended up with him in the kitchen. After culinary school at Johnson & Wales University in Rhode Island, he interned at Chicago's Tru. That experience introduced him to his mentor, Chef Rick Tramonto.

Pandel soon left Chicago for New York City, where he cooked at the famed Café Boulud. "That's where I really learned how to cook," he says. Daniel Boulud's café is also where Pandel picked up his butchering skills.

After six years in New York, he returned to Tru and helped open Tramonto's Osteria Via Stato. He worked on cookbooks with Tramonto and helped him with marketing and private dinners.

But Pandel craved a return to the kitchen. In 2008, he opened The Bristol (the Old English word for "a meeting place under a bridge"), a neighborhood eatery north of downtown Chicago that's known for its charcuterie and farm-to-table focus.

"We have a lot of freedom," Pandel says of his ingredients. "Tons of freedom, which is really nice. Once you have a heart steak, you'll probably crave that more than a ribeye."

Clearly, Pandel is a guy who knows ingredients. It's high praise when he says the "best pigs we've seen at this restaurant" come from Scott Hasselmann's farm.

Hasselmann, who grew up in the Chicago suburbs, is the son and grandson of mushroom farmers. "I spent all my free time over there; my weekends, after school, my whole life growing up," Hasselmann says. "I always had animals—rabbits, goats, pigs, chickens."

He majored in agriculture at Western Illinois University and went on to serve in the Peace Corps in Nicaragua, where he also worked on farming programs (and met the woman who would become his wife). He went to graduate school and studied sustainable international development before returning to Nicaragua.

But the Hasselmanns came back to the Chicago area to raise their children. And, of course, Hasselmann started farming. It's in his blood.

"I just did it as a hobby for years," he says. "And now, the last couple of years, we went full time."

The farm in Marengo, Illinois, about 50 miles from downtown Chicago, is home to pigs, chickens, cattle, and sheep. The Hasselmanns raise chickens both for eggs and for meat.

"I just like animals," Hasselmann says. "I'm good at raising animals. Everyone's good at something. I love working with animals; it's not even really work for me. I'm doing this and I'm making a living at it. How cool is that?"

Still, it's not an easy job. There are no days off, even when the farmer is under the weather. "The worst is when you're down with the flu or something," Hasselmann says. "It's all hand labor. It's not push-button farming. It's high labor. That's why the end product is so good."

The Hasselmanns have a handful of restaurant clients and sell quite a bit at area farmers' markets.

"Chris [Pandel] has been my best customer," Hasselmann says. "He's just a pleasure to work with. I really appreciate what he's doing. I'd love to have ten restaurants like his. He respects the farmer, and all he can, he uses from farmers. If I didn't have somebody like Chris buying my pigs, I'd have to sell them on the commodities market. It's just great he values what we do.".

Pork Loin Tonnato

From Chris Pandel of The Bristol

Serves 2

8 oz. brined pork loin and belly (brine recipe follows)
4 tbsp. fresh tonnato sauce (recipe follows)
1 c. fresh arugula
Splash of lemon juice
1 tsp. extra-virgin olive oil
Salt and pepper, to taste
1/2 oz. Pecorino Romano cheese, shaved

Roll and tie the brined belly and loin and roast at 300°F until the internal temperature is 145°F. Allow the roast to come to room temperature and chill in the refrigerator.

Slice the pork loin and belly very thinly and dress with tonnato sauce. Dress the arugula with lemon juice, olive oil, salt, and pepper. Shave the Pecorino into the salad. Arrange the salad atop the pork loin.

PORK LOIN BRINE
6 qt. water
2 c. kosher salt
1 tbsp. curing salt #2 (available in specialty shops and online)
1 c. sugar
2 garlic cloves
5 rosemary sprigs
10 peppercorns
1 bay leaf
10 parsley stems

Dissolve kosher salt, curing salt, and sugar in water. Blend garlic, rosemary, peppercorn, bay leaf, and parsley with water. Chill. Brine pork loin and belly three days before roasting.

TONNATO SAUCE

Makes about 3 cups

4 oz. good-quality tuna poached in olive oil
2 c. garlic aioli (recipe follows)
3 tbsp. rinsed capers, chopped
3 tbsp. red onion, minced
1/2 tsp. fresh marjoram, minced
1/4 c. fresh parsley leaves, chiffonaded
1 tbsp. red wine vinegar
1 anchovy fillet
1/2 lemon, juiced
Kosher salt and fresh-cracked black pepper, to taste

Combine the tuna and aioli in food processor and blend until smooth. Remove mixture from processor and into mixing bowl. Fold in all remaining ingredients and adjust seasoning as necessary.

AIOLI

Makes about 3 1/2 cups

7 egg yolks
Dash of white vinegar
3 c. vegetable oil
Garlic, to taste, grated with a microplane
Salt, to taste

Whisk egg yolk and vinegar together in bowl and gradually add oil, whisking constantly until all of the oil is incorporated and the mixture is emulsified. Add in grated garlic and salt, to taste.

Nena's Slow-Cooker Pulled Pork Tacos

From Scott and Nena Hasselmann
of Hasselman Family Farms

Makes about 15 tacos

3 lb. pork shoulder roast, preferably Berkshire
1 1/2 tsp. pork seasoning
1 clove garlic, crushed
1 can pineapple chunks, in juice
1 tsp. melted butter
4 tbsp. cilantro, chopped
1/4 c. chopped onion
1 pkg. shredded cheese (Mexican style)
1 small pkg. flour tortillas

Sprinkle pork seasoning on both sides of roast. Crush garlic clove and rub it on both sides of roast.

Place roast in slow cooker and add can of pineapple and juice. Cook in slow cooker on low for 7 hours.

Take the roast out of the slow cooker and cut into strips. Remove fat. Place pulled pork and all the juice and pineapple in a skillet. Add butter, cilantro, and onion and simmer for about 15 minutes, or until some of the juice has cooked away. Add a pinch of salt and pepper.

Next, grease a frying pan with 1/2 tbsp. of butter. Fill a flour tortilla with pulled pork and sprinkle cheese. Roll the tortilla and cook until light brown on each side. Repeat, using all of the meat and tortillas.

winter

Chicago winters get a bad rap. Sure, they're cold and snowy. Downright miserable at times.

But those bitter days provide the perfect excuse to cozy up by the fire and warm up with some comfort food. Slow-roasted pork. Sausage hand pies.

Cheesecake. Don't worry about calories.

You need them for warmth.

Chalkboard

Chef Gilbert Langlois
Slagel Family Farm

Gilbert Langlois had been a chef his entire adult life. But he had never given much thought to using organic, local, or sustainable foods until his son, Owen, was born about five years ago.

That's when he became concerned about growth hormones in milk and the overabundance of corn syrup in processed foods.

After receiving the keys to his restaurant, Chalkboard, just two days after his son's birth, he realized the food at his new upscale eatery could and should reflect that growing concern.

"I realized, I don't have to ask anybody," Langlois says of owning his first restaurant. "I can support farmers and they can be nice to me."

Now, he lists foods from a variety of area farmers on his menu. The menu changes daily and is, of course, handwritten on a large chalkboard.

"I get bored with food very quickly," he says.

Langlois, who grew up in Mokeena, Illinois, remembers growing up with a mom and grandmother who were "always cooking," he says. He recalls standing in the kitchen, arms outstretched, being used as a human drying rack for fresh-made pasta.

By the time he went to culinary school at Joliet Junior College, he was already working in restaurant kitchens. His cooking has taken him to restaurants all around Chicago and also to New Orleans.

But he is enjoying the freedom he has at Chalkboard. He likes experimenting with unusual cuts of meat and "weird variety stuff" like sweetbreads, tongue, shanks, and liver.

"It's a tough sell," Langlois says. "It's easy to sell halibut. It's hard to sell tongue. My biggest complaint about American dining is that people are cut-selective."

He buys much of his meat from Slagel Family Farm in Fairbury, Illinois. He remembers fondly when LouisJohn Slagel asked him if he'd like to buy a goat.

"I told him, 'You have to walk through the front door with your product, so people can see." Langlois says. "I want people to know what we're buying."

LouisJohn Slagel's family has been raising livestock for generations in central Illinois. But when he finished college about five years ago, he decided to change things up a bit on the farm. Now, in addition to raising the livestock, the Slagels run their own slaughterhouse.

"There's a lot of advantages to it," Slagel says. "Mainly, we have control over everything. There's no third party. We have a lot more flexibility as far as cutting stuff to order for various customers. Also, we can do whatever works for our schedule to be able to offer stuff as fresh as possible."

As a boy, Slagel always loved the animals on the farm and enjoyed working with livestock. He grew up with a clear understanding of the difference between pets and livestock.

"I just kind of have to realize that's what the animals are for," he says. "It's not my favorite job in the world [slaughtering animals]. But I feel like it's something that has to be done."

Slagel grew up in a large family of six brothers and six sisters. Many of his siblings work on the farm, and his parents continue to as well. Slagel's uncle is the head butcher.

The number of animals sold each week varies, Slagel says. On average, he slaughters one or two steers, one or two head of cattle, about 100 chickens, and some goats and sheep, depending on the orders.

When he first took over the business, Slagel started calling chefs mentioned in *Chicago* magazine to tell them about his product. That's how he first connected with Langlois.

"I got lucky to work with chefs from the beginning who had a good reputation," he says. "For a while, I continued to call chefs and try to push our product. But after the first year or so, we started having enough chefs. The product started marketing itself."

Roasted Pork Tenderloin
with Sauteed Farm-fresh Vegetables and Ancho-Corn Sauce

From Gilbert Langlois of Chalkboard

Serves 4

1/2 of a dried ancho chili
1 c. hot water
1 c. corn kernels
4 white potatoes, cut into large cubes
1 pork tenderloin, about 2 lbs.
2 tbsp. kosher salt
2 tsp. sugar
1 tsp. lavender flowers
8 shitake mushrooms, sliced
1 tbsp. butter
1/4 c. white wine
1/2 c. chicken stock
Salt, to taste
1 whole apple, sliced

Preheat oven to 350°F.

Prepare ancho-corn sauce by soaking the dried chili in hot water for 10 minutes to soften. Puree corn and chili in blender, with a little of the soaking water, if necessary, to help liquefy the sauce. Heat sauce in a small saucepan and simmer until thickened and reduced. Keep warm.

Sauté cubed potatoes in a hot skillet just until browned, place in a roasting pan, and put in oven and cook until tender. Keep warm.

Rub pork tenderloin with salt, sugar, and lavender flowers. Roast until internal temperature reaches 160°F. Let pork rest, covered.

Sauté mushrooms in butter with wine, stock, and salt, to taste. Cook until liquid is reduced and mushrooms are tender.

To serve, place a bed of roasted potatoes on each plate. Top with sautéed mushrooms, apple slices, and sliced pork tenderloin. Drizzle with sauce.

Beef Tongue Tacos
with Avocado-Cilantro Puree and Lime Crème Fraîche

From Gilbert Langlois of Chalkboard

Serves 8

- 1 fresh beef tongue, 2–2 1/2 lbs.
- 2 carrots, roughly chopped
- 2 celery stalks, roughly chopped
- 2 white onions, roughly chopped
- 4 garlic cloves, smashed
- 1 tbsp. black peppercorns
- 1 bay leaf
- 1 tsp. cumin
- 1 tbsp. butter
- 4 avocados, peeled and cubed
- 2 bunches cilantro, roughly chopped
- 2 sweet onions, sliced thin
- 1 c. crème fraîche (or sour cream)
- Zest of 2 limes
- 2 heirloom tomatoes, diced
- 16 (or more) corn tortillas, preferably homemade

Put beef tongue in a large stock pot, along with carrots, celery, onions, garlic, peppercorns, bay leaf, cumin, and enough water to cover. Bring to a boil and simmer for 6 hours, until tender. Remove tongue from liquid. When it's cool enough to handle, peel off the skin. Plunge the tongue into ice water to cool it completely before cutting into thin slices. Sauté the sliced tongue in butter at medium-high heat until crisp.

Make the avocado-cilantro puree by adding the cubed avocado and chopped cilantro to a blender with a splash of water. Blend until smooth.

Sauté the thinly sliced sweet onion in a sauté pan over medium until lightly caramelized.

Combine the crème fraîche (or sour cream) with the lime zest. Reserve.

To serve the tacos, top warmed tortillas with cooked beef tongue, diced tomatoes, and caramelized onions. Drizzle with the avocado-cilantro puree and serve with the lime crème fraîche.

David Burke's Primehouse and the James Hotel

Chef Rick Gresh
Swan Creek Farm

Things looked bleak for farmer George Rasmussen in the spring of 2009, after he lost his truck, trailer, and generator to fire while on the way to Chicago for deliveries.

Rasmussen, who raises cows, pigs, chickens, ducks, and rabbits on his Swan Creek Farm in Hillsdale County, Michigan, didn't know how he could continue his business.

But then dozens of Chicago chefs—some who weren't even Swan Creek customers—banded together to put on a fund-raising farm-to-table dinner, as well as an auction of their services.

Their efforts raised enough money to buy Rasmussen a new Chevy rig, complete with a navigation system.

"It was hard for me to say 'thank you' without breaking down," Rasmussen says. "That was so phenomenal.

"With all the chefs I have a very, very great rapport. We talk about how they prepare something and I get to taste it and be part of it. It's an absolutely wonderful, rewarding thing."

Rick Gresh, the chef at David Burke's Primehouse and the James Hotel, joined those efforts. Gresh, who used to sneak pickled beets out of the jar from his grandmother's cellar, grew up in a family committed to gardening, composting, and preserving. (He still keeps an overflowing garden at his suburban home, bursting with rhubarb, tomatoes, asparagus, strawberries, onions, carrots, beets, peppers, melons, and herbs.)

"It was just a way of life I grew up with," Gresh says. "You'd rarely see a jar of Smuckers at my parents' house."

He started cooking for himself at a young age and remembers asking for a wok for his thirteenth birthday, before going on to study French classics at the Culinary Institute of America. He now oversees all of the food at the steakhouse and all of the banquet, catering, and other dining operations at the hotel.

"We're a big from-scratch operation," Gresh says. "For the steakhouse, we own our own bull who sires the beef and we age it in-house. We're not the old fuddy-duddy, wood-paneling steakhouse. We're modern and cool and hip, and we're a little edgy."

But in a hotel operation, he must try to accommodate guests from other parts of the country and world. And if a guest requests melon in February, he must supplement with nonlocal produce.

"The Midwest is hard with its growing season, obviously," Gresh says. "But when it's kicking, we're probably at least 60 percent local."

Plus, he says, "I do a lot of the same things I did with my parents, pickling and preserving."

And at such a large food-service business, he must be ever-mindful of cost. He chose to stop using a small, local egg purveyor in favor of a larger (but local) producer to save money.

"It's heartbreaking on one level, but it's still a business," he says.

Rasmussen was born in Denmark and later moved to Canada, where he worked on dairy farms. He moved to Detroit and started studying fine arts when he discovered he had a knack for drawing some of the illustrations he saw in newspapers. He began working as a freelance fashion illustrator for an ad agency. (Rasmussen declined to give his age but says "drinking raw milk and raw honey and eating really good food just about all my life" has kept him looking about twenty years younger than he actually is.)

For the past decade, he has been farming some 140 acres at Swan Creek ("no produce, all protein," he says).

He takes pride in what he produces, beaming about a Chicago chef who was once asked how he makes such wonderful chicken. "Buy them from George," Rasmussen says was the reply.

Rasmussen only sells directly to chefs, not at the farmers' markets. He is glad to see such an emphasis on local foods at Chicago restaurants.

"It does require a higher price on the menu, but it will also be a lot healthier thing for people eating in the city," he says.

Slow-roasted Pork Shoulder

Slow-roasted Pork Shoulder

with "Mole Broth" and Tortilla Flan

From Rick Gresh of David Burke's Primehouse and the James Hotel

Serves 4–6

- 1 onion, chopped
- 4 garlic cloves
- 2 ancho peppers, soaked for 30 minutes in warm water, stemmed and seeded
- 1 tbsp. black peppercorns
- 1 carrot, chopped
- 1 celery stalk, chopped
- 3 qt. chicken stock, divided

- 5 lb. bone-in pork shoulder
- Salt and pepper, to taste
- 1/2 vanilla bean, split and scraped
- 4 sprigs thyme
- 4 sprigs marjoram
- 1/2 c. almonds
- 1/4 bunch cilantro, chopped

Preheat oven to 325°F.

In a blender, combine onion, garlic, drained ancho peppers, black peppercorns, carrot, and celery. Add enough of the stock to make a smooth mixture.

Season pork with salt and pepper. Sear in a hot pan over high heat until deep golden brown. Remove meat, set aside, and turn flame down to medium. Add blended liquid and remaining stock, along with the vanilla bean, to the searing pan. Boil. Reduce heat to simmer for 30 minutes. Add thyme, marjoram, and seared pork, cover, and place in preheated oven for 3 hours. Add the almonds and cilantro and return to oven for approximately 1 more hour, until the pork is tender. Remove pork from pan. Reduce sauce to thicken, if necessary. Adjust seasoning, strain, and serve over the pork.

TORTILLA FLAN

- 3 poblano peppers, charred over an open flame
- 10 oz. tomatillos
- 2 garlic cloves
- 1 bunch cilantro
- 4 eggs
- 1 qt. heavy cream
- 1 bag corn tortilla chips, plain
- Vegetable spray, as needed
- 2 c. mild cheddar cheese, shredded
- Salt and pepper, to taste

In a blender, puree peppers, tomatillos, garlic cloves, cilantro, eggs, and cream until smooth. Pour over chips in a large bowl and mix together well. Spray a large oven-proof pan with cooking spray. Add alternating layers of the chip mixture and cheese. The mixture should be wet. Add more cream if it seems dry. Preheat oven to 325°F. Set aside pan, covered, at room temperature for 40 minutes. Add additional cream if the mixture seems dry. Cover and bake for about 30 minutes, until set.

62 Degrees Celsius Duck Egg

with Spicy Asparagus, Watercress, and Parmesan Cheese

From Rick Gresh of David Burke's Primehouse and the James Hotel

Serves 2

- 2 duck eggs
- 1 bunch asparagus, blanched, shocked in ice water, and split in half, cut into 1 1/2-in. lengths
- 1/4 tsp. red chili flakes
- 1/2 c. watercress
- Kosher salt and pepper, to taste
- 1 lemon, juiced
- 1 oz. olive oil
- 2 tbsp. Parmesan cheese

Place the duck eggs in a water bath held at 62°C (144°F) for 1 hour. In a bowl, toss the asparagus, chili flakes, watercress, salt, pepper, lemon juice, and olive oil. Place the salad onto a plate. Remove the egg from the water bath and lightly cut through the shell, just to weaken the membrane. Gently crack the egg and separate the shell in two. Season with salt and pepper and place on top of the salad. Garnish with Parmesan cheese.

Hoosier Mama Pie Company

Chef Paula Haney
C & D Family Farms

Pastry chef Paula Haney had worked at some of Chicago's finest dining establishments, crafting inventive desserts. But she had a more humble after-dinner craving: A nice slice of pie.

"My husband and I went looking for it," Haney recalls, "and we couldn't find it. Why can't you have a shop that just makes pie?"

Beyond her personal quest for a tasty piece of pie, Haney considered it from a historical point of view.

"I was concerned we were going to lose this knowledge, that people were going to lose what a real pie tasted like," she says.

Haney took matters into her own hands. She quit her restaurant gig and started making pie full-time.

The Hoosier Mama Pie Company (she and her husband both grew up in Indiana) began out of a shared-used commercial kitchen, allowing Haney to start selling her pies to coffee houses and at farmers' markets. About three years later, she had earned enough to open her own pie shop.

Pies are relatively simple creations, so the quality of each ingredient really stands out. That's why Haney likes to use as much local produce as possible. She tries to keep her pies as seasonal as possible but admits "there would be a riot if we didn't" offer apple pie year-round.

Her grandparents and in-laws are farmers, so she understands the hard work and commitment that goes into the products.

"Farmers have an amazing work ethic," she says. "We're always struggling to get to the market on time in the morning. But the farmers have been there since 3 a.m."

Haney began serving savory pies at her shop recently. "Mostly I think because we got hungry. We're in here with fruit all the time," she says.

Farmer Crystal Nells and her husband, Dan, have a similar story of making a major life change. The two had been living in Chicago, working as electrical contractors, when they decided they needed a different lifestyle. They both wanted jobs that would allow them to work primarily from home.

So they packed up and moved a couple of hours away, to 15 wooded acres in Knox, Indiana. They decided to raise livestock, and after considering cows and chickens, they settled on pigs.

They'd never raised pigs (or animals of any kind) before, but they read a few books and toured some large confinement hog farms.

"We were disgusted by it," Nells says. "We decided we wanted to do pigs—outside where they belong. Pigs are incredibly smart and very social."

Now the Nells have 125 pigs to feed and scratch behind the ears. And when the animals get to 250–280 pounds, they go to the butcher.

That's always a tough day for her husband, Nells says.

"Every single time we take the pigs to the butcher, it's a major argument because he doesn't want to part with anybody," she says.

So how does a hog farmer meet up with a pie baker?

Haney had been selling her pies at the Green City Market. She was there the day Crystal Nells showed up as a guest vendor, and the two wound up next to each other.

Nells didn't know it, but Haney had been thinking about creating some savory pies. Once the pastry chef tried some of Nells' sausage, she knew she'd found a winner. Haney buys 30 pounds a week of the pork-apple-sage sausage for her pies that are stuffed with sausage, potatoes, onions, crème fraîche, and Granny Smith apples.

"I love working with the farmer," says Haney, who also sources much of the fruit for her pies from area growers. "It's a lot of fun. I know exactly where our food comes from. Aside from being local and supporting the farms, it's nice to know Crystal's animals are not being mistreated. It's nice to know they're being treated well."

Nells jokes that she got into farming to work from home, and now she's hardly ever home. She sells her frozen pork products at farmers' markets around Chicago, getting up at 2:30 a.m. on market days to make the trip up to the city.

Cream Cheese Dough

Cream Cheese Dough

From Paula Haney
of Hoosier Mama Pie Company

We love this dough and use it all year long to make hand pies with seasonal ingredients from the farmers' market. Use either a stand mixer or food processor, but be careful: This dough can be rough on noncommercial mixers.

1 1/4 pounds unbleached all-purpose flour
1/4 tsp. kosher salt
1/4 tsp. granulated sugar
1 lb. unsalted butter cut into 1-in. cubes
1 lb. cream cheese cut into 1-in. cubes
1–2 egg whites

Combine the flour, salt, and sugar in a medium bowl with the cream cheese and butter and toss until the butter and cream cheese is coated with the flour mixture. Chill the entire mixture for 1 hour. Transfer to the bowl of a food processor or stand mixer. In a food processor, pulse until the butter and cream cheese pieces are the size of large peas and the mixture is sandy. In a stand mixer, combine slowly by turning the machine on and off.

Next, if using a food processor, process just until the mixture forms a ball. If using a stand mixer, turn the machine to a high speed and mix for 20–30 seconds. Turn dough out onto a floured work surface and knead until smooth. Divide into two balls and flatten into disks. Wrap each disk in plastic and rest in the refrigerator at least 1 hour.

To assemble: Take one disk of dough out of the refrigerator. Let stand at room temperature for 5 minutes. Working quickly, roll dough 1/8-in. thick. Using a pastry cutter or jar lid, punch out the dough into 4–5-in.-diameter circles. Transfer to parchment-lined sheet pan or cookie sheet and place in the freezer. Repeat process with the other half of the dough, placing circles on a second cookie sheet.

Take the first cookie sheet of circles out of the freezer. Prepare a third parchment-lined cookie sheet. Transfer a few circles at a time to the new cookie sheet and brush lightly with egg whites. Place 2 heaping tbsp. of filling in the center of the circle. Fold the dough in half over the filling to form a half moon. Crimp the edge with the tines of a fork to seal.

If the dough becomes too soft to work with, return first cookie sheet to freezer and switch to circles from the second cookie sheet. If the circles are too cold to be pliable, warm them between your hands for a few seconds or let stand at room temperature until workable. You may have to do this several times before all the pies are filled. Return assembled pies to the freezer for at least 1 hour before baking.

To bake: Preheat oven to 400°F (350°F in a convection oven). Arrange hand pies 1 in. apart on a parchment-lined sheet pan or cookie sheet. Bake 20–25 minutes until pies are golden brown. Let stand on the baking sheet for a few minutes to firm. Transfer to a plate with a fork or offset spatula. Pies should still be warm. Serve warm. Makes approximately 40 hand pies.

Sausage Hand Pie Filling

From Paula Haney
of Hoosier Mama Pie Company

1 lb. C & D Family Farms breakfast sausage, browned in a
  saute pan over medium heat
1 small yellow onion, minced
1 tsp. fresh sage, finely chopped
2 tbsp. parsley, chopped
2 oz. Brunkow Little Darling cheese, grated
Kosher salt and freshly ground pepper, to taste

Combine all ingredients. Fill hand pies as directed on page 137.

Pork-Apple-Sage Pie Filling

From Paula Haney
of Hoosier Mama Pie Company

1/4 c. olive oil
1 c. onions, halved and sliced thin
2 c. 1-in. cubed russet potatoes
1 lb. C & D Family Farms breakfast sausage
2 c. of 1-in. cubed firm tart apples (Granny Smith,
  Empire, Mutsu)
2 tbsp. grainy mustard
2 tbsp. sage, finely chopped
6 tbsp. crème fraîche
1/2 tsp. of salt
Fresh-ground black pepper, to taste
Prepared pie dough (recipe on page 137)
1 egg, beaten

Heat the olive oil in a sauté pan. Add onions and sauté until soft and just starting to brown. Add potatoes, reduce heat to medium low, and sauté until potatoes can be pierced by a fork. Transfer potatoes and onions to a medium bowl. Place sauté pan back on heat and add sausage, breaking it up with a spatula. Sauté until it is lightly browned and cooked through. Using a slotted spoon, transfer browned sausage to bowl of potatoes and onions. Add cubed apples, mustard, sage, crème fraîche, salt, and pepper. Mix to combine and let cool thoroughly before using.

This mixture can be used in hand pies or to make one 9-in. classic two-crust pie.

For hand pies, follow hand pie assembly instructions. For the 9-in. pie, using your favorite pie dough recipe, roll out two 14-in. rounds of pie dough. Place one in a 9-in. pie pan, being sure to press it down into the bottom corners of the pan. Mound filling mixture in center of pan and smooth to the edges of the lip of the pie tin. Center the second round over the pie filling. Working around the pie, roll the edges of the two pie crusts under and tuck up onto the rim of the pie pan. Next crimp the edges between your thumb and finger. Brush the top of the pie, including the crimp, with a beaten whole egg. Cut 4–6 steam vents and place in freezer for at least 1 hour.

Preheat oven to 400°F (350°F convection). Place pie on cookie sheet and place in oven. Bake 40–60 minutes. When done, pie crust will be baked to a medium golden brown and filling should be heated through with some bubbling through the vents. Serve warm.

Pork-Apple-Sage Pie Filling

The Publican, Blackbird, avec, and Big Star

Chef Paul Kahan

Burton's Maplewood Farm

Visit one of Paul Kahan's four Chicago restaurants, and you'll see plate upon plate of evidence pointing to his commitment to local, seasonal food.

But his vision sprouted years before Blackbird, avec, Publican, and Big Star. Decades ago, before becoming one of the most respected chefs in Chicago, Kahan hitchhiked to Chez Panisse—Alice Waters' San Francisco monument to homegrown, in-season foods—on a quest to meet the good-eating guru. The visit helped instill him with passion for seasonality and for farmers' markets. And, over the years, the two have become friends.

"Now I've met her and cooked for her and hung out with her," Kahan says.

Kahan grew up in his dad's deli and smoked-fish factory in Chicago. He remembers grabbing pickles out of the barrel and enjoying Dr. Brown's soda and Jays potato chips at the deli. He remembers glimpsing his first sturgeon at the factory, a 200-pound beast that was "like a sea monster," he recalls.

"All kinds of things like that really made an impression on me," he says.

But that's not the path upon which Kahan began. He first received a degree in applied computer science from Northern Illinois University. When he met the woman who would later become his wife, she introduced him to her friend, who was a pastry chef.

Kahan was intrigued and started working, from the bottom up, in the kitchen of Erwin Drechsler, chef-owner of Chicago mainstay erwin. Drechsler "was really passionate about seasonality," Kahan says.

Kahan went on to spend nearly four years in the "almost utopian" kitchen of Rick Bayless, who continued to reinforce the importance of in-season foods and of farmers' markets.

"The first market of the year is really such a huge point of excitement," Kahan says. "All the chefs have been hibernating all winter. For me, I always walk the market and see if there's anything new."

It's understandable Kahan was delighted to meet Tim Burton, of Burton's Maplewood Farm. Burton and his wife, Angie, produce high-quality maple syrup on their land in Indiana, about five-and-a-half hours from the Green City Market.

The Burtons were new to the market—and the Chicago restaurant scene—when approached by Kahan in 2009. In fact, Tim Burton referred to Kahan's famed Blackbird restaurant as "Blackberry" and suggested he put a country-style wooden "syrup hutch" in the upscale dining room to display the maple syrup. Burton and Kahan laugh about that now.

The hutch may not go with Blackbird's tony decor, but the restaurant goes through plenty of the farm's syrup. At the Publican, Kahan bastes pork belly with it before finishing the dish with butter and a little more maple syrup.

"We sell a ton of it," he says.

In just a year, the Burtons have been schooled in the Chicago restaurant scene. Their syrup is used in dishes at some of the city's hottest spots, including The Bristol, North Pond, Table Fifty-Two, the Signature Room at the 95th, Atwood Café, and many others.

"Our hopes were that we could reach out to some notable and progressive chefs at restaurants," Tim Burton says. "And, knock on wood, we've been very fortunate. These guys are genuinely interested in where the food comes from."

In their first year, the Burtons, who also own a systems-integration business, made about 200 gallons of syrup. Now, three years later, they're producing some 2,000 gallons.

Angie Burton's family has been tapping trees for maple syrup for about 200 years. Tim Burton says they've long been intrigued by that rich family history and "the lost social aspect of making maple syrup."

Gathering sap, boiling, reducing, and bottling the syrup is so labor intensive that it was often an excuse for family and friends to gather and accomplish the task. The Burtons often invite chefs and others down to the farm to experience the process. Each March, they host the National Maple Syrup Festival.

The syrup season in southern Indiana runs from mid-January to the first two weeks of March, give or take a couple of weeks on either side. Sap runs from the roots to the canopy, just as blood runs to the extremities in humans. Warm days and extra-cold nights brings on the best sap flows.

Sap is consolidated into a tank in the sugar house, where it flows into an evaporator—an oil-driven boiler system that reduces and caramelizes the sap into thick, rich syrup. It takes about 43 gallons of sap to produce 1 gallon of syrup.

"I'm still in awe of this," Tim Burton says.

Maple-glazed Pork Tenderloin
with Wax Beans and Marcona Almonds
From Paul Kahan of Publican

Serves 4

5 c. water
3 tbsp. salt
6 tbsp. sugar
2 1-lb. pork tenderloins
3/4 c. maple syrup (preferably Grade B)
1/4 c. sherry vinegar
1 Fresno chili
2 tbsp. plus 1 tsp. extra-virgin olive oil
4 tbsp. butter
1/2 lb. stemmed wax beans, cut in half
1/4 c. Marcona almonds, coarsely chopped
1 tsp. fresh rosemary leaves

Make brine by combining the water, salt, and sugar. Rinse the meat and pat dry. Place pork in the brine and use a plate to keep the meat submerged. Cover and refrigerate overnight or up to 2 days. A couple of hours before cooking, remove the tenderloins from the brine. Rub and massage the meat as you rinse it under cold water. Press dry between towels. Refrigerate until about 15 minutes before cooking.

Preheat the oven to 425°F.

In a blender, combine the syrup, vinegar, and chili. If you prefer less heat in the glaze, remove the seeds from the chili.

Rub the tenderloin with 2 tbsp. olive oil. Over medium-high heat, quickly sear the meat in an oven-proof skillet. Place the skillet in the oven and roast for about 20 minutes.

Remove the pan from the oven and flip the tenderloins in the pan. Add butter to the pan and let it melt. Incorporate the maple glaze into the pan before the butter browns. With a large spoon, baste the meat with the glaze continuously for up to 5 minutes, turning the meat if it gets too dark. Let the meat rest 5–10 minutes out of the pan.

While the meat is resting, blanch and shock the wax beans, remove from ice water, and pat dry. In a sauté pan, heat 1 tsp. extra-virgin olive oil over high heat until just smoking. Add the almonds, rosemary, and wax beans and turn heat to medium until beans are heated through.

Carve meat into thick slices and top with the wax bean mixture.

Terzo Piano

Chef Meg Colleran Sahs
Capriole

Judith Schad was a stressed-out mom with three young children, working on her doctoral dissertation in Renaissance literature, when she knew she needed a change. She had spent summers growing up on her grandparents' small hobby farm in southern Indiana, where "they just grew everything and canned and preserved everything," Schad says. "That was a pretty idyllic introduction to farming."

Schad stopped working on her degree and, in 1977, moved her family to her husband's great-great-grandfather's farm in southern Indiana. A neighbor suggested she get a goat. And then she got another.

"I caught the farm bug first, and the goat bug next, and then the cheese bug," she says. "Like city people would, we fell in love with goats because they were cute and fun. There was so much milk, I didn't know what to do with all of it."

Schad took a quick cheese-making class, bought a book called *Cheese-Making Made Easy*, and started experimenting with cheese-making in her kitchen in 1980.

Schad now owns 525 goats and is one of the country's premier makers of farmstead goat cheese. She produced nearly 85,000 pounds of her Capriole goat cheese (named after a goat's playful leap) in 2009. The company makes several varieties of fresh and aged cheeses by hand, using only the milk produced on her farm.

Capriole started its production with plain, milky white goat cheese extruded into a log, but Schad has expanded and become more creative over the years as she has honed her craft.

"There was so much demand to have variety," she says.

Schad sells her cheese in rounds, logs, pyramides, and other sizes. Favorites include surface-ripened varieties such as Sofia (which is layered with ash), Piper's Pyramide (a dense, creamy cheese sprinkled with paprika), and the flavorful O'Banon (aged in bourbon-soaked chestnut leaves).

"We're slaves to the milk," she says. "We're making cheese every day because of the milk."

Goats are milked twice a day. The milk is then pasteurized before a small amount of culture and rennet are added. The mixture ferments overnight and is ladled into molds. Aged cheeses go into a cave to ripen

Capriole's business took off in the late 1980s when restaurants became interested in Schad's high-quality products.

"The chefs were the beginning," she says. "That was the evolution. And retail came next. Once people began to eat it in restaurants, it grew that way."

Now you can find Capriole cheese on menus around Chicago, including at the bright and airy Terzo Piano restaurant in the new Modern Wing of the Art Institute of Chicago.

Meg Colleran Sahs, the restaurant's chef di cucina, serves Capriole on a cheese platter, but she also stuffs it into a lamb burger and uses it to top a pork-belly flatbread. The restaurant goes through about 20 pounds of fresh Capriole goat cheese each week.

"It's pretty delicious," Colleran Sahs says.

Colleran Sahs, who grew up in the Chicago suburbs, first became interested in restaurant management in high school. Fresh out of college, she took a marketing job in New York, but, she says, "I was pretty miserable. I knew it wasn't what I wanted to do."

She enrolled in the French Culinary Institute, landed a cooking internship in France, and eventually started working at the De Gustibus Cooking School at Macy's in New York City. It was there that she met Tony Mantuano, one of the big-name chefs brought in by the school for demonstrations.

Mantuano is the chef at Spiaggia, a favorite of the Obamas, and is now also the executive chef at Terzo Piano.

When Colleran Sahs moved back to Chicago, she found a place at Spiaggia. While working there, she took a "break" to do a one-month internship at Chez Panisse.

"I knew I had to go there to feel complete in my culinary training," she says. "I was blown away. Everything they brought in was from a local farm. Everything. It was so cool to see the best of the best of the best produce."

At Chez Panisse, cooks used fat sparingly and let the flavor of the fresh ingredients shine, which was a technique markedly different from the classical French cooking she learned in school.

"From that experience, I have been totally changed as a chef," she says.

Given the growing season in the areas around Chicago, it's almost impossible to be as local as Chez Panisse, Colleran Sahs says.

"We're moving every day more and more toward it," she says. "In the beginning, you do your best. You have to get the restaurant open. We sourced as much locally as we could and filled in the gaps. As we've moved forward, every day we're moving more toward being more local and more sustainable."

Flatbread

with Goat Cheese, Crispy Pork Belly,
Dried Apricots, and Lime

From Meg Colleran Sahs of Terzo Piano

DOUGH

Makes one flatbread

    1 1/4 c. all-purpose flour
    1 tbsp. kosher salt
    2/3 c. warm water, divided
    1/4 oz. fresh yeast

Combine the flour and salt. In a small mixing bowl, dissolve the
yeast in 1/3 c. warm water. Slowly add the water/yeast mixture into
the flour, along with remaining 1/3 c. water.

Mix the dough in a stand mixer fitted with a dough hook for 10
minutes, adding additional flour if the dough is too sticky and not
holding together.

Move the dough to a large oiled mixing bowl and cover tightly with
plastic wrap. Let sit for at least two hours, or overnight, at room
temperature.

A premade pizza dough can also be used in place of this recipe.

PIZZA SAUCE

Yields enough for 4 flatbreads

    2 c. tomato pulp
    2 tbsp. extra-virgin olive oil
    1 tsp. kosher salt

Combine all ingredients in a blender until smooth. This sauce can
keep in the refrigerator for one week.

PORK BELLY

    1/2 skinless pork belly (about 5–6 lb.)
    2 tbsp. black peppercorns
    2 tbsp. juniper berries
    1/3 c. kosher salt
    3 tbsp. dark brown sugar
    2 tbsp. curing salt (pink salt)
    1/2 tsp. ground nutmeg
    3 garlic cloves, minced
    4 bay leaves, torn into small pieces
    2 tsp. fresh thyme leaves
    1 tbsp. fresh rosemary leaves
    1 qt. chicken stock

Rinse and dry the pork belly with paper towels. Place the belly in a baking dish.

In a spice grinder, pulverize the black peppercorns and juniper berries. Move to a medium mixing bowl.

Add salt, brown sugar, curing salt, ground nutmeg, minced garlic, bay leaves, and chopped thyme and rosemary. Combine well.

Rub the entire belly with the curing mixture, making sure to get cure on all sides. Any additional cure can be put below or on top of the belly in the baking dish.

Place another dish or a plate on top of the belly, and weigh the belly down with something heavy and food safe.

Move to the refrigerator and allow the belly to cure for 1 day. Turn the belly over, weigh it down, and let cure for at least 1 more day. The pork belly can be cured for up to 5 days.

Preheat the oven to 300°F.

Take the belly out of the refrigerator and rinse off the cure. Move to a clean baking dish or roasting pan. Pour chicken stock around the belly, and cover the dish with aluminum foil.

Braise the pork belly in the oven until fork-tender, and then cool completely in the liquid.

When ready to use, remove the belly from the braising liquid and move to a clean cutting board. Cut the belly into 1/2-in. square pieces.

Heat a large sauté pan on medium heat. Add the cubes of pork to the pan to crisp them, and render out of the fat. When crispy, move to a strainer resting over a bowl to drain off the fat. The fat can be reserved for another use.

This recipe will yield enough for about 12 flatbreads. The pork belly is very versatile and also great in scrambled eggs, omelets, or on its own, sliced in larger pieces and crisped in a sauté pan.

FLATBREAD

 1 batch dough (recipe on previous page)
 All-purpose flour for rolling
 1/2 c. pizza sauce (recipe on previous page)
 1 tsp. kosher salt
 1/2 c. crispy pork belly (recipe on previous page)
 1/4 c. dried apricots, cut into strips
 2/3 c. Capriole goat cheese
 2 tsp. cilantro leaves, washed and chopped
 1 tsp. green onion, washed and cut into thin strips
 Sea salt
 Juice of 1 lime wedge

Preheat the oven to 500°F. If a pizza stone is available, place the stone in the oven to heat.

On a clean work surface, sprinkle some all-purpose flour and move the dough to the floured surface. Using your hands, press down on the dough to release air bubbles. Rotate the dough pressing out into a circle. The resulting dough should be 10–12 in. in diameter.

Pour the pizza sauce onto the dough and spread with a pastry brush. The sauce should be in a thin layer all the way to the edges of the dough. Sprinkle with kosher salt.

Sprinkle the crispy pork belly and dried apricots on the pizza. Finish by dolloping the goat cheese all around the dough. Make sure to place the cheese near the edges.

If no pizza stone is available, move the dough to a clean sheet of parchment paper and move directly to the oven rack, placed in the middle of the oven. If a stone is available, skip this step and move the dough directly onto the stone.

Cook for 8–10 minutes, or until the crust is crispy on the bottom and the cheese has melted. If a premade pizza dough is used, the cooking time will decrease.

Move the cooked pizza from the oven to a cutting board and finish with the cilantro, green onion, sea salt, and fresh lime juice. Cut and serve.

Red Beet and Celery Salad
with Pyramide Goat Cheese

From Meg Colleran Sahs of Terzo Piano

Serves 4

1 tbsp. plus 1 tsp. kosher salt
2 large red beets
3 stalks celery, cleaned
1 tsp. celery seed
1 tsp. kosher salt
1/3 c. high-quality red wine vinegar
Sea salt, to taste
Fresh-ground black pepper, to taste
3/4 c. extra-virgin olive oil
1 tsp. parsley, chopped
1 tsp. chive, chopped
1 tsp. tarragon, chopped
Baby arugula for garnish, optional

Fill a medium saucepan two-thirds full with water and add 1 tbsp. kosher salt. Bring to boil, turn down heat slightly to a simmer, and add the beets.

When the beets are soft throughout (check with a paring knife), about 20 minutes depending on size, remove from the water and let cool slightly.

Using paper towels, remove the outer skin from the beets. Place in refrigerator to cool completely.

Using a knife, cut the celery lengthwise into 1/4-in.-thick pieces, on a bias. If not using immediately, store the shaved celery in water to keep fresh and crisp.

In a spice grinder, combine celery seed with 1 tsp. kosher salt. Reserve for later use.

In a medium mixing bowl, combine red wine vinegar, sea salt, and black pepper. Slowly whisk in the olive oil to emulsify. Stir in the chopped herbs and season to taste.

When ready to assemble, cut the beets into small wedges. Place in a small bowl. Add vinaigrette to coat, and season to taste. Add salt and pepper if necessary.

In another small bowl, add celery and salad dressing. Sprinkle in some of the celery salt and season to taste.

To assemble the salad, place the beets on the bottom of the serving dish. Top with celery. Place the cheese around the beets and celery. Finish with a sprinkle of the celery salt on the edge of the dish for garnish. Place baby arugula around the top of the salad, if desired.

Goat's Milk Cheesecake
with Hazelnut Shortbread Crust

From Megan Neubeck, pastry sous chef at
Terzo Piano

CRUST

Makes enough for 2 cheesecakes

3/4 c. hazelnuts
3 c. bread flour, divided
1 1/2 c. unsalted butter, softened
3/4 c. organic cane sugar
1 tsp. salt
1/2 tsp. vanilla

Preheat the oven to 350°F.

In a food processor, combine the hazelnuts and 1 1/3 c. bread flour until pulverized. Pass the nut flour through a sifter. Add the remainder of the bread flour and sift one more time.

Combine butter and sugar in a mixer with the paddle attachment on medium speed. Add salt and vanilla.

Turn down the mixer speed to low and add all the flour. Mix until just combined.

On a lightly floured surface, roll dough out into a disk 1/8 in. to 1/4 in. thick.

Press the dough into a 10-in. springform pan about halfway up the sides of the pan, making sure to push the dough into the corners. Place the crust onto a sheet tray and move to the oven.

Bake for 10–15 minutes, until lightly browned. Remove from the oven and cool completely.

FILLING

12 oz. Capriole fresh goat cheese
16 oz. fresh cream cheese
1 1/4 c. organic cane sugar
2 tsp. lemon zest
2 tsp. lemon juice
1 1/2 tsp. vanilla
Pinch sea salt
4 eggs
Boiling water

Preheat the oven to 325°F.

In a mixer with the paddle attachment, combine the goat and cream cheeses on medium-low speed. Add sugar, lemon zest and juice, vanilla, and salt. Add eggs one at a time, making sure to scrape down the sides of the bowl. Fully incorporate each egg before adding the next.

Once the batter is well combined, pour into the cooled shell. Wrap the outside of the entire springform pan with two layers of aluminum foil around the bottom and outside of the pan. Place the foil-wrapped cheesecake in a large baking dish. Pour hot, preferably boiling, water around the outside of the cheesecake, about 2 in. from the top of the baking dish. Carefully move the entire baking dish into the oven and bake for 45–60 minutes. When the cheesecake is ready to remove, there should be a 4-in. round spot in the center of the cheesecake that is still shaky. Cool the cheesecake in the water bath for 1 hour, and then move to the refrigerator to chill completely. Wrap and save until serving. The cheesecake will keep for 3–5 days.

Goat's Milk Cheesecake

Vie

Chef Paul Virant
Dietzler Farm

Like many chefs who have a strong commitment to local, seasonal foods, Paul Virant grew up with an appreciation of the garden.

"I was fortunate enough to have grown up in an area where we had land," says Virant, the chef/owner of Vie in the Chicago suburb of Western Springs, Illinois. "We always had a big garden. We had chickens and a couple pigs. All that stuff kind of adds up to understanding seasonality."

He remembers his Polish grandfather making homemade sausage. And now, he says, "Sausage and charcuterie is a huge part of what we do at the restaurant. We do have the antique sausage stuffer that was my grandfather's. We use it at the restaurant."

He also recalls his mother canning and pickling produce grown on the farm, techniques that have become staples at Vie. One of the mantras in his kitchen is, "Taste of the season, preserved."

"It was very much Midwestern comfort food," says Virant, whose earliest professional food experience came as a soda jerk at Six Flags amusement park in St. Louis, near where he grew up. He has come a long way since then.

Over the years, his seasonal, rustic dishes at Vie have earned Virant and the restaurant a slew of awards. In 2007, *Food & Wine* magazine named Virant one of the country's best new chefs, citing as the reason for the award that Virant "wants to get his customers as excited as he is about the supreme local and seasonal ingredients in his Western European-accented menu."

He first met farmer Michelle Dietzler when she brought samples of her grass-fed beef to the restaurant several years ago. The meat has had a place on his menu ever since.

"We get half sides at a time," Virant says. "We do all the fabricating. It comes in four quarters and we break it down into subprimal cuts from there. We use every part."

Like Virant, Dietzler grew up in a family bound to the land. For the Dietzlers, the cattle farm began as a "summer hobby," she says.

"My dad didn't want his kids eating genetically modified beef," Dietzler says. "He decided that's what he wanted to do with his land, for his family to eat good beef."

Dietzler didn't think much about the farm until several years ago, when she was working in Chicago for a website that reviewed spas and salons. She tired of the job, and about five years ago, she quit and turned her efforts to the family farm.

"I figured I'd help my family out for a little while and see if I could start selling this beef at farmers' markets," she says.

Business took off like a runaway bull. Dietzler beef is now in about fifty restaurants and counting around Chicago.

"I really love what I do," Dietzler says. "This is part of my childhood too. It's been really exciting. I didn't go into this having any expectations."

Since Dietzler maintains a small operation, she is able to customize her products for the chefs with whom she works. "Now, they can dream up whatever they want," Dietzler says. "We can feed [the cows] a certain ration. We can age them a certain number of days."

When the economy stumbled in recent years, she started getting requests for more unusual, and inexpensive, cuts of meat, such as beef cheeks and hearts.

"Organ meat is the hot thing," Dietzler says. "When I started this, people had a lot of disposable income. When the economy took a dive, the restaurants weren't interested in the fancy tenderloin. Now, everyone is fighting over the brisket or the inexpensive oxtail.

"It's so rewarding now to go to a restaurant and see our name on the menu."

Beef Liver Mousse

From Paul Virant of Vie

1 lb. beef liver
Milk, for soaking the liver
2 shallots, sliced
2 tbsp. cognac
2 tsp. mustard powder
1 tsp. ground coriander
1 tbsp. brown sugar
1/2 tsp. cayenne pepper
1/2 tsp. black pepper
1 1/2 tsp. kosher salt
1/4 tsp. pink salt or curing salt
6 oz. pork fat back, diced
1 egg plus 1 yolk
5 oz. whipping cream, hot

Soak liver in enough milk to cover. Let rest overnight in refrigerator. Drain liver and marinate with shallots, cognac, spices, and seasonings overnight in refrigerator.

Preheat oven to 350°F.

Blanch fatback in boiling water for 30 seconds (to soften the fat). Blend liver with marinade and eggs in a food processor. Add hot fatback, blend, and while the machine is running, slowly add the hot cream. Pass mixture through a basket strainer. Pour mixture into a greased ovenproof dish, cover with foil, and cook in water bath. Bake until internal temperature reaches 150°F. Cool overnight in the refrigerator and serve with crusty bread, pickles, and preserves. By using the curing salt, the mousse will keep for two weeks in the refrigerator.

Spicy Beef Skirt Steak Salad

From Paul Virant of Vie

Serves 4 as an entree salad

- 1 whole dry-aged beef skirt steak, trimmed, about 1 lb.
- 1 lemon, juice and zest
- 1/2 sweet onion, sliced
- 2 garlic cloves, minced, divided
- 1/4 c. plus 2 tbsp. extra-virgin olive oil, divided
- 2 tbsp. red wine vinegar
- Salt and pepper, to taste
- 4 plum tomatoes, washed, cored, and halved lengthwise
- 2 hot peppers (jalapeño works well), washed and halved lengthwise
- 1/4 c. grapeseed oil
- 1 c. day-old bread cubes, large diced
- 1/4 lb. arugula, washed
- 1 c. fresh-picked herbs (cilantro, parsley, chives)
- Parmigiano-Reggiano cheese, grated or shaved, to taste

Marinate beef in lemon zest, onion, 1 clove garlic, and 1 tbsp. olive oil overnight, covered, in the refrigerator.

Combine remaining garlic, red wine vinegar, and 1/4 c. olive oil. Add salt and pepper, to taste. Reserve.

Preheat oven to 400°F. Toss tomatoes and peppers in 1 tbsp. olive oil, season with salt and pepper, and roast for 30 minutes. Reserve.

Heat the grape seed oil in a sauté pan over medium-high heat. Fry bread cubes until crisp. Season with salt and pepper. Reserve. Preheat grill. Season skirt steak with salt and pepper and grill to medium rare, about 3–4 minutes. Allow the meat to rest.

Rough-chop tomatoes and peppers. In mixing bowl, combine arugula, herbs, croutons, peppers, tomatoes, and onion. Toss with reserved vinaigrette, season with salt and pepper, and divide onto four plates. Slice steak and place on top of salad. Garnish with grated or shaved cheese, serve.

Restaurant Directory

Aria
200 North Columbus Drive
Chicago, IL 60601
312-444-9494
www.ariachicago.com

Bleeding Heart Bakery
1955 West Belmont Avenue
Chicago, IL 60657
773-327-6934
www.thebleedingheartbakery.com

Browntrout
4111 North Lincoln Avenue
Chicago, IL 60618
773-472-4111
www.browntroutchicago.com

The Butcher & Larder
1026 North Milwaukee Avenue
Chicago, IL 60647
773-687-8280
www.thebutcherandlarder.com

Chalkboard
4343 North Lincoln Avenue
Chicago, IL 60618
773-477-7144
www.chalkboardrestaurant.com

Chilam Balam
3023 North Broadway Street
Chicago, IL 60657
773-296-6901
www.chilambalamchicago.com

David Burke's Primehouse
616 North Rush Street
Chicago, IL 60611
312-660-6000
www.davidburke.com

The Dining Room at Kendall College
900 North Branch Street
Chicago, IL 60642
773-312-7522
www.kendall.edu

Floriole
1220 West Webster Street
Chicago, IL 60614
773-883-1313
www.floriole.com

Frontera Grill and Topolobampo
455 North Clark Street
Chicago, IL 60654
312-661-1434
www.fronterakitchens.com

Gourmet Gorilla
877-219-3663
info@gorillakids.com
www.gourmetgorillainc.com

Hoosier Mama Pie Company
1618 1/2 Chicago Avenue
Chicago, IL 60622
312-243-4846
www.hoosiermamapie.com

HotChocolate
1747 North Damen Avenue
Chicago, IL 60647
773-489-1747
www.hotchocolatechicago.com

Lula Cafe
2537 North Kedzie Boulevard
Chicago, IL 60647
773-489-9554
www.lulacafe.com

Nacional 27
325 West Huron Street
Chicago, IL 60654 312-664-2727
www.n27chicago.com

Naha
500 North Clark Street
Chicago, IL 60654
312-321-6242
www.naha-chicago.com

Nightwood
2119 South Halsted Street
Chicago, IL 60616
312-526-3385
www.nightwoodrestaurant.com

North Pond
2610 North Cannon Drive
Chicago, IL 60614
773-477-5845
www.northpondrestaurant.com

Prairie Fire
215 North Clinton Street
Chicago, IL 60661
312-382-8300
www.prairiefirechicago.com

Prairie Grass Cafe
601 Skokie Boulevard
Northbrook, IL 60062
847-205-4433
www.prairiegrasscafe.com

Province
161 North Jefferson Street
Chicago, IL 60661
312-669-9900
www.provincerestaurant.com

The Publican
837 West Fulton Market
Chicago, IL 60607
312-733-9555
www.thepublicanrestaurant.com

Signature Room at the 95th
Hancock Observatory
875 North Michigan Avenue
Chicago, IL 60611
312-787-9596
www.signatureroom.com

sola
340 N. Clark St.
Chicago, IL 60654
773-327-3868
www.sola-restaurant.com
(The sola location at 3868 North Lincoln Avenue will now become ohana, also owned and operated by Chef Carol Wallack. Ohana will be more budget-friendly than sola but will have the same farm-to-table focus.)

Terzo Piano
159 East Monroe Street
Chicago, IL 60603
312-443-8650
www.terzopianochicago.com

The Bristol
2152 North Damen Avenue
Chicago, IL 60647
773-862-5555
www.thebristolchicago.com

Uncommon Ground
3800 North Clark Street
Chicago, IL 60613
773-929-3680
and
1401 West Devon Avenue
Chicago, IL 60660
773-465-9801
www.uncommonground.com

Vie
4471 Lawn Avenue
Western Springs, IL 60558
708-246-2082
www.vierestaurant.com

Local Food Resources

The **City of Chicago** runs farmers' markets on Tuesdays, Wednesdays, Thursdays, Saturdays, and Sundays from May to October in more than twenty neighborhoods around the city. For a schedule of markets, log on to www.explorechicago.org.

Green City Market, Chicago's only year-round farmers' market, was founded in 1998 by Abby Mandel. Green City has been called the country's "best sustainable market" by chef Alice Waters. From May to October, the market operates on the south end of Lincoln Park. In the winter, it runs in the Peggy Notebaert Nature Museum. www.chicagogreencitymarket.org, 773-880-1266.

FamilyFarmed.org works to improve the production, marketing, and distribution of locally grown foods. The nonprofit group hosts the annual FamilyFarmed EXPO at Navy Pier, one of the largest yearly local food events in the Midwest. www.sustainusa.org.

Seeding Chicago is a website that explores "how urban agriculture is taking root and transforming lives." It is run by several Chicago journalists who are passionate about local food and social justice. www.seedingchicago.com.

Slow Food Chicago works to support food that is good for the people who eat it, good for the people who grow it, and good for the land upon which it grows. The organization also works to improve access to local foods. www.slowfoodchicago.org

The **Chicago Food Policy Advisory Council** consists of farmers, planners, and city officials. It works to improve access to safe, healthy, sustainable food for all Chicago residents. www.chicagofoodpolicy.org, 773-486-6005.

Chicago Rarities Orchard Project (CROP) hopes to create community rare-fruit orchards throughout the city. The organization is working with city officials to acquire land for planting. www.chicagorarities.org, crop@chicagorarities.org

Purple Asparagus is a nonprofit group that puts on events focused on encouraging good eating for families. The group organizes health fairs and expos aimed at children and families, cooking classes, and other educational activities. www.purpleasparagus.com

The Local Beet: Chicago is a web-based publication giving practical tips for organic and sustainable eating. *The Local Beet* also publishes guides to finding community-supported agriculture farms (CSAs) and other local-food resources. www.thelocalbeet.com.

About the Author and Photographer

Heather Lalley is an award-winning journalist with a passion for food. After earning a journalism degree from Northwestern University, she spent a decade as a reporter for *The Spokesman-Review*, the daily newspaper in Spokane, Washington. Her work has also appeared in the *Chicago Tribune*, *Time Out Chicago*, and on the Associated Press wire, among other outlets. She graduated from Chicago's Washburne Culinary Institute in spring 2011, with a degree in baking and pastry arts. Lalley chronicled her two years in culinary school on her *Flour Girl* blog. She loves baking bread and creating dishes with her farmers' market finds. Lalley lives in Chicago with her husband and young son.

Brendan Lekan is a renowned food photographer with a natural eye for capturing the beauty of food. He has spent extensive time honing his skills, working with high-profile clients like Kraft Foods, and has developed a sharp eye for food and beverage through his regular contributions to *Time Out Chicago* magazine. Lekan is the direct descendant of acclaimed butchers, and he is an avid fisherman. His life-long exposure to the food making process and his love of the outdoors is reflected in not only these images, but all of his work.

Acknowledgments

Thank you to each of the farmers and chefs in this book, who work early mornings and late nights to grow and prepare local foods for the rest of us to enjoy. Despite their busy schedules, they found time to further support local food by being interviewed, being photographed, and providing the recipes that make up this book. Also thank you to all of the Chicago-area farmers' market founders and directors, who have brought together growers and cooks (both restaurant and home) in a rich, vibrant, ever-blossoming local-eating community.

I must also thank my editor, Kari Cornell at Voyageur Press, for enlisting me to take on this wonderful project and for her hard work in shaping the end result. Thank you also to the super-talented photographer Brendan Lekan, who logged many miles in his car and many frames on his camera to make this book the beauty that it is. Much gratitude also to my ever-persistent assistant, Jason Smith, who made dozens of calls to chefs to track down recipes.

And, of course, I could not have written this book without the unwavering support of my own personal cheering section: my husband, Frank, and my son, Nick. Thank you, guys. I love you.

Index